All Seriousness Aside

Stories from the back page

The Critics Aren't Raving!!!

Because they haven't read this book yet. But here's what readers have to say about *All Seriousness Aside:*

"I enjoy every column, but this one, *Of Bats and Men*, was so damned funny that the occupant of the office next to mine came in to see why I was laughing so hard. (She actually thought I was wheezing and she was worried she'd find me unconscious on the floor.)"
Marc S. Berris,
Segal, Roston & Berris

"Bill has the courage to write what most people think but would never feel comfortable admitting. ... Even my children look forward to reading his columns."
Reneé Hammes-Briggs,
President, Uncommon Professionals Inc.

"When my non-lawyer wife insists each month on reading a column in a law-related magazine before I do, and then either laughs or cries, it's clear these columns are extraordinary!"
Allen Saeks,
Leonard Street and Deinard

"Bill White's columns demonstrate that a light touch is often most revealing."
Jule Hannaford,
Kelly, Hannaford & Battles

"If there's humor to be found in the routine of life, Bill finds it, and if there's an engaging way to write about it, Bill does it with wit, charm, insight and hilarity. You read, you relate, and you laugh and learn."
Stephen R. Bergerson,
Fredrikson & Byron

"Bill White's columns are beautifully rendered vignettes of ordinary, everyday life that simultaneously touch your heart and your funny bone."
Dan Carr,
CEO, The Collaborative

"Laugh. Learn. Live better. That's what will happen when you read these columns. Bill White is one of my favorite writers."
John Rosengren,
award-winning author of Blades of Glory

"You will enjoy this collection and read it often..."
Michael Tewksbury,
Tewksbury & Kerfeld, P.A.

"A humorous, poignant collection of essays that captures the imagination."
Gregory L. Wilmes,
North Central Equity LLC

"A wonderfully human piece."
John Dornik,
Mackenzie & Dornik

"Bill's thoughtful and humorous commentary on everyday life will brighten anyone's day (even a lawyer's)!"
Dennis B. Johnson,
Chestnut & Cambronne

"When I get my new issue of *Law & Politics,* the first thing that I do is read Bill White's last page. It's like eating dessert first!"
George S. Holzapfel,
Lasher Holzapfel Sperry & Ebberson

"Bill White's columns continuously reflect humorous and humane insights into life, law, and other lunacy."
Marshall H. Tanick,
Mansfield Tanick & Cohen

"I have saved most of Bill White's columns over the past four to five years and take them out occasionally to brighten up a particularly gloomy day."
Mike Trucano,
Dorsey & Whitney

All
Seriousness
Aside

Stories from the back page

William C. White

Mill City Press, Inc.
212 3rd Avenue North, Suite 570
Minneapolis, MN 55401
612.455.2294
www.millcitypublishing.com

ISBN - 1-934248-68-1
ISBN - 978-1-934248-68-3
LCCN - 2008935146

Cover Design by Miranda Moos
Typeset by Peggy LeTrent

Printed in the United States of America

In memory of my dad, Robert L. White,
the funniest and greatest guy I've ever known.

Contents

Foreword

In 1992, when Bill White started using his "All Seriousness Aside" column in *Minnesota Law & Politics* to take a Seinfeld-like look at his own life, something magical happened. A world as universal—and funny—as that of Lake Wobegon was created, only this was not some imaginary small Minnesota town, this was real life. We followed his bachelor days and his courtship with Linda and then their marriage as if we were all his best friends. And the readers loved it. For me, it was more like tough love. As the editor of *Law & Politics*, I had to resist White's monthly pleas to please let him skip his column this month—he was always way too busy to write it; and then my job was to see that the always-in-late column didn't come in *too* late to print, an event only barely avoided almost every month for more than a decade. It was, as you're about to see, all worth it.

Steve Kaplan
Editor
Law & Politics
and *Super Lawyers*

Introduction

In the late 1980s, I was a frustrated, restless lawyer. At the time, I had this vague creative urge that I felt would not be met by practicing law. After a couple of years of hand-wringing and introspection, I somehow worked up the foolish courage to leave the practice. Like jumping out of an airplane, unsure if I remembered to put on a parachute, I went into a professional free fall.

Miraculously I landed safely in the publishing business. Without any experience or training, I found myself running a magazine called *Minnesota Law & Politics*, which we launched in 1990. With me in charge, we were like children without parental supervision. We broke all the rules.

Instead of creating a dry, legal trade journal that lawyers *had* to read, we created an offbeat, cheeky publication that lawyers *wanted* to read. The magazine oftentimes more closely resembled *Mad* magazine than the *Harvard Law Review.* Our slogan—"Only our name is boring"—captured the essence of the magazine.

As publisher, I ran the business side of things. But on the first and last pages of the magazine, I was able to take care of the creative itch that drove me out of law in the first place.

Working with photographer Larry Marcus, I created covers featuring buck naked politicians, bungee-jumping lawyers, and professional wrestlers; and then there were the parodies— *Cosmopolitan* magazine, *Sports Illustrated*'s swimsuit issue, Norman Rockwell paintings, Calvin Klein ads and politicians taking a wide stance in the men's room. It was all a lot of fun.

On the back page, I was supposed to write a publisher's letter. But I soon realized I couldn't do this and keep a straight face. So, I decided to use the space to write humorous bits and pieces about law and politics. I named the column "All Seriousness Aside," a phrase I remember Steve Allen using on his 1970s talk show as he transitioned from one silly bit to the next.

But after a year or so, the jokey schtik format wore thin. In 1991, on a whim, I began to write stories about the very ordinary events in life: going to the dry cleaner, getting a haircut, filling the car with gas—anything but the serious stuff of law and politics.

This book is a collection of some of those stories. They were written over a sixteen-year period and are arranged for the most part in the order in which they appeared in the magazine. The stories are creative non-fiction; on occasion I needed to condense events to fit onto one page in the magazine, or change the identity of individuals I didn't want to name. Other than that, these stories are pretty much the way it was, exactly as I remember.

WCW

Target: Right on Our Money

On my sixth lap around the Target parking lot I spot them. An elderly couple has just loaded their trunk with bags. I move into position and wait. I know I shouldn't do this but I've been driving around this parking lot so long I'm running low on fuel.

The gentleman, who looks like Wilfred Brimley, sees me waiting. I give him a take-your-time wave and smile. But apparently he's not the smiling type. He snorts indignantly. As long as their car is there, it's *their* parking spot.

I lightly drum the steering wheel and in my rearview mirror see that a car now waits behind me. Won't be but a few seconds until I can pull into the spot. As soon as they pull out of the spot, I can park and we can all be on our way.

All right. Wilfred and his wife have their doors open. "C'mon, you can do it," I whisper to them as I spot a second car behind me in the rearview mirror. Like felled trees, the couple slowly falls into their seats. I can see them huffing and puffing as they struggle to arrange coats and legs and torsos and purses. Oops. Mother must be sitting on the seat-belt buckle. She fusses with the belt before Wilfred attempts to help.

Okay. We're buckled in, ready for takeoff. But before he starts the car, Wilfred runs through a checklist like this was a NASA mission. A third car now joins the queue.

Wilfred starts the car. But wait. Apparently there's technical difficulty in the cockpit. Wilfred decides to abort the launch. T-minus four cars behind me and holding.

A fundamental rule of the universe is being played out: As the line of cars behind you increases, the speed at which the people you wait for decreases in direct proportion.

Should I just move on? The guy behind me looks deranged with rage. But I can't leave. I've committed to this spot.

Apparently Wilfred and his wife have passed away because I see absolutely no movement in the car. Just as I'm about to give up, the vehicle lurches backward, then stops. Both gray heads bob simultaneously. Captain Brimley now inches his way out of the spot. Careful, careful. Despite the fact he's a good five yards from the nearest anything, he moves with the care of one performing eye surgery. I notice the line of cars in the next aisle over. I realize they are waiting for us. I hate people who do what I'm doing. Damn! This parking space has turned me into someone I despise.

Finally, mercifully, the couple clears the spot. I've got a parking spot at Target! I'll be home for Christmas after all! But I am not here to Christmas shop.

I come merely to purchase one item and one item only: a shower curtain. And I would not choose this time of year to shop for a shower curtain were it not absolutely necessary.

I don't know exactly how old my shower curtain was, but it was mighty stiff. In fact it was so brittle it was beginning to crumble each time I touched it and I was getting tired of sweeping up after each shower.

I grab a cart large enough to carry a recliner.

The store is packed. Zombie shoppers look right through me with glazed expressions. It's like *Night of the Living Dead* pushing shopping carts. Children whine, couples snap. 'Tis the season to shop until you crack. I head straight to housewares determined to resist the seduction of the happy red signs proclaiming unbelievable savings. Whatever you need to run the infrastructure of your life—wiping, drying, cooking, cleaning, buffing, whatever—it's all here in long neat aisles. And now looking down on the row of Tidy Bowl and coffee makers are the wholesome black and white images of Donna Reed and Jimmy Stewart. *It's a Wonderful Life* used to be a movie. Now it's an ad. Every time the cash register bleeps, an angel gets his wings.

I don't know much about shower curtains. I think about them rarely, about as often as I might think about, say, the Battle of Hastings.

But there is a lot to know. There are dozens of styles to choose from and prices vary wildly.

For some reason, I can't remember the color of the tile in my bathroom, so I settle on a modestly priced, nondescript curtain and liner and head to the checkout anxious to get out of this place.

As I stroll through the aisles I spot a bargain on Crest I just can't pass up. I pick up a couple of tubes. Then I spot big savings on lightbulbs, and Lysol. And while I'm here, I could use Kleenex and socks and underwear and batteries and film and scotch tape and Jergen's and Old Spice and Prell and Charmin, all at amazingly low prices. My purchases fill four bags. Even though I racked up great bargains, I spent three times more than I intended.

I walk out into the gray afternoon, laden with

my non-Christmas bags. This year, the spirit of Christmas is not with me. Maybe it would be different if these bags I carry were full of gifts for others.

Cars circle the lot like vultures. As I toss the bags into the trunk, a poacher slowly pulls up behind me and waits.

I get in the car. Looking in the rearview mirror I study the face of the driver. It's a mother with a child in the backseat. She looks guilty and nervous as if she's in danger of being arrested for blocking traffic.

I pause for a moment, then wishing her Merry Christmas, I quickly bestow upon her the gift of my empty space.

The Sitter

It's Saturday afternoon. I lie on the couch with the channel changer on my stomach, my metabolism slower than the golf commentary on television. I was thinking about maybe getting up and scrounging for chips or something, but that involves walking all the way to the kitchen. I think I should rest a bit longer before undertaking such work.

The phone rings. My arm falls off the couch and sweeps the phone off the hook. I reel it in by the cord, and drag the receiver to my ear. "'Lo," I gurgle.

"Bill, you're going to kill me." It's my sister. "We can't find a sitter."

She has to be desperate. I'm probably the last person in the state she's called. My daily experience with kids is limited to driving past a day-care center on my way to work. I'm probably more qualified to be an air-traffic controller than I am to babysit her five children.

I'm tempted to feign a seizure, or pretend I'm removing a pork roast from the oven for a dinner party I'm having for sixteen—anything.

"But if you have big plans for the evening, I understand," she says. "We can stay in." Sure. She and her husband haven't been out since Ronald Reagan was president. I'm their last hope.

"Um, sure-re," I say, the word caught in my throat like a hairball. With a voice weak from the strain of false enthusiasm, I tell her how much I'd love to babysit.

I arrive at my sister's house just before six. My sister has that perfumed smell of Saturday night that I remember as a kid meant liberation from the parents. In high heels, she steps over a doll house and a hockey stick and points out phone numbers, bottles and formula. She and her husband take turns apologizing and thanking me. I wave it off like babysitting is no big deal. I pick up the 6-month-old Mary Claire, and walk them to the door.

"You kids go have a great time. Heck, stay out 'til 7:30, 8 o'clock if you want."

"Thanks again, Bill. We'll be home around midnight." That's six hours. About twice the length of a marathon. I try to say good-bye, but

Mary Claire has hold of my lower lip. "You kids be good," my sister yells over her shoulder.

The door shuts. The kids scatter like mice. They have their work cut out. There's a house to destroy, siblings to be tortured, and a babysitter to disobey. Mary Claire and I stare at each other. Then the terrible truth dawns on her. Mommy's gone and I'm here. This is a rotten trade. Her face tightens into a frown like she just ate a sour grape. She launches into a scream. I try talking to her. "Doo, doo, there, there." Doesn't work. I try walking her, rocking her. Nothing works. Then I remember: How do adults solve their problems?

The bottle works like a charm. She grunts with pleasure as she urgently inhales the formula; her tiny, pink hands grab for empty air before she pokes herself in the eye. While I'm feeding the baby, Emily and Carolyn, ages 7 and 5, conduct a bragging competition. They model new dresses, perform gymnastics, show me artwork, and tell me stories. I say "wow, gee, really!!??" a couple hundred times while trying to keep the nipple from going in Mary Claire's ear.

I check on their brother Kyle who's downstairs in the playroom. The room is a broken ankle waiting to happen. If it rolls, it's on the floor: footballs, baseballs, golf balls, marbles, skateboards. He's off in the corner talking to himself, announcing play-by-play to an imaginary game of hockey. He wheels and takes a slap shot, sending a tennis ball whizzing past my ear.

Upstairs the kids are watching a video they've seen sixty times. They lie on their stomachs, their heads arched back, looking up at the screen three feet away, positions that would paralyze an adult. Their wide eyes drink in the blue flickering light. Connor, the 3-year-old, looks at the screen from corner to corner, his mouth wide open like a bird waiting to be fed.

There's a smell. I look around. Is something cooking in the kitchen? Then I see Mary Claire. She grimaces like a power lifter, then relaxes with a smile. This is the moment of truth. My greatest challenge as a sitter: the diaper change.

I open the little plastic package. My head snaps back in surprise. The prodigious load is perhaps half the size of the child. Her legs pumping like a frog, she somehow gets a hold of my hair and threatens to pull me into her creation. I pry her fingers loose, but now she's got me by the nose. Compared to this, the Exxon Valdez was an easy cleanup. I go through half a box of Handi Wipes making sure every fold of fat is clean. Except for the fact I put the diaper on backwards, the operation is a success.

Downstairs, Connor has fallen asleep in front of the set. I pick him up. He feels like he's grown in the last hour. His head hangs back. A string of drool follows us halfway out of the room. I lay him into bed, he snorts and rolls over. That was easy. One down, four more to go.

Getting the girls to brush their teeth is not easy. Emily decides it's comedy night. "Uncle Bill, I forgot how to brush my teeth." Picking up a hairbrush she says, "I can't get this in my mouth!" Her smile shows off a random display of teeth, half missing, the other half still grade-school jagged.

Bedtime negotiations with the girls are as complex and trying as any labor-management dispute. Their demands are endless and unreasonable: the number and length of stories to be read; where I have to sit when I read; the amount of light that must be let into the room before I can shut the door. I try persuasion, threats, scolding, reverse and double-reverse psychology. It is only the blessing of fatigue that works. Finally they fall asleep, their bodies sprawled sideways across their beds. I sneak back in the room and carefully tuck them in. Then I hurry off to quiet Mary Claire who's wailing in her crib.

Four minutes before midnight, the house is finally silent. I sit in the darkness and stare. I hear the tires on the driveway.

"Oh, no sweat!" I lie. "I was born to be a sitter! Please, let me babysit again, soon, please!"

My sister and her husband laugh at what a

liar I am. For them tomorrow means more diapers, more prodding, and more scolding. Each of the five will be fed, washed and put to bed every day for the thousands of days that it takes.

According to the headlines, humankind is in trouble. Crime and war and injustice. But every decent parent on the planet is a superhuman, and every day is a miracle of patience. Diapers, bottles, love—somehow, we are sustained.

High School Daze

The guidance counselor frowns as he studies my transcript. His head tilted back slightly, he peers through reading glasses perched on the end of his nose. Then, like someone who's studied the menu and is ready to order, he tosses my records on his desk and states his conclusion.

"Well, I guess we won't be attending Carleton now, will we?" he says, fixing his gaze on me over the top of his glasses. His mouth forms a smile in which his eyes do not participate.

I have no idea what Carleton is. The only Carlton I know is a low tar cigarette. But I gather this is some sort of guidance counselor joke based on my transcript, a masterpiece of mediocrity, a sea of C's interrupted only by the occasional D and less frequently by a B.

It's less than a month until high school graduation. And I still haven't applied to college. But there is a good reason for this. Filling out an application would take some discipline, initiative and follow-through, things I'm completely incapable of. I have moved through my high school years like a liquid, flowing in a path of least resistance, with only gravity to guide me. No direction of my own. Just whatever.

"Where do you think you'd like to go to school?" he asks.

I dunno, I respond, in a teenage monotone, slouching ever lower in the chair. My legs bounce restlessly and my eyes stream across the ceiling.

"What subjects do you enjoy?"

I shrug. My eyes wander out the window. Then, without looking at the counselor, I blurt out something I'd been thinking about ever since the day I overslept and almost missed taking my SATs. "Maybe I'm not cut out for college."

"Oh, nonsense," he says. He slides a junior college brochure across the desk and starts talking about admission requirements. But I don't hear a word he says because I think I've made up my mind. I don't want to go to school ever again. I've been thinking about the Navy. Ah, yes, the Navy. Travel, adventure, salt-water spray in the face, and best of all, it's not college! As my counselor rambles on, I make up my mind. I'm joining the Navy.

I walk out of the counselor's office that Friday morning in early May at peace finally knowing the direction my life is headed. Next week is prom. Then I'll fake my way through finals, grab my diploma, and then be off, never to set foot in a school again. And tonight, and every night until graduation, I will go out and smoke and drink my way into a higher state of high school oblivion. But first, I have a high school baseball game to play. No big deal.

***

The baseball rises into the afternoon sky and for a moment it seems to stop, suspended in blue, before making its slow descent back to earth. I race across the infield, calling for the catch. Just as I reach out for the ball, all becomes slow motion.

My left leg hooks the leg of a teammate who is running past me and attempting to step out of my way. My body goes forward, but my leg doesn't come. There is a sound like a well-hit baseball.

I flip and when I land, I look at my leg in disbelief. My left lower leg is bent to the side at a right angle. A bone pokes through my uniform and blood pours onto the grass. It's a Joe Theismann break before there was a Joe Theismann break. I'm like the scarecrow in *The Wizard of Oz* trying to put his body back together. I grab my lower leg, throw it straight and let out a scream that sounds like my body is possessed.

Pain from a new region of the imagination overtakes me. I lie back, looking up at the sky, fighting off the urge to panic or faint. Teammates and coaches arrive on the scene, but all quickly circle away, their hands to their mouths. I hear subdued whispers of disbelief around the infield. "Oh my god. Oh jeezus."

Nobody seems to know what to do. The thought occurs to me that if somebody doesn't do something, I might bleed to death right here, near second base, beneath the Edina water tower.

But then out of the stands comes Bob Carlson, our third baseman's father. He's been present at every game since Little League. The smell of his pipe is as much a part of those games as the smell of the leather of a mitt.

He bends down over my leg, applies just enough pressure to stop the bleeding. He looks like he'd sound like the Crusher, but his voice is a baritone as mellow as aged scotch. "You're gonna be all right," he assures me.

Suddenly, my fear subsides. There is no pain, just the thought, "Wow. I've never broken a leg before. Cool." As adrenaline races through my body, all is bliss. Broken leg. Big deal. Like nobody ever broke a leg before? La la, into shock I go.

For the next month, during what should have been the wildest time in my life, I lie in bed, pins in my leg, cast up to my hip. The torture of stillness. No distractions. Time to think. Forced to reflect. I'm so bored I actually read a book. Then another. And another. Life takes a turn.

I never join the Navy. But had that pitch not been thrown, or that ball not hit? How different life might have been.

A quarter century to the day later I write this, and every slow motion detail of that day remains in my head. Maybe it's a miracle, or just blind luck that we all survive being 18, and somehow end up who we are.

Uphill Struggle

Shortly after Mass begins, my furnace kicks on. I am roasting under layers of sweaters, turtlenecks and long underwear, and to save precious time on the slopes, I've already got my ski boots on.

Church is the last place I'd be if my dad didn't make us go, but as long as I'm here I pray for a quick Mass. My heart sinks, however, when old Father DeMuth takes the altar and slowly genuflects, creaking like an old rocking chair.

When Mass finally ends, I double-clump with each step in my ski boots as I hurry out of the church to the car. Six of us kids pile into the green 1965 Vista Cruiser station-wagon, which is now dusted white with road salt. It's cold enough that the snow squeals under the turning tires, yet my dad is oblivious and keeps the window rolled partway down. "The fresh air will do you good, kids."

A half hour out of Minneapolis, my brother Bob has brother Jim in a choke hold. Jim's flailing arms catch dad's eyes in the rearview mirror. "Boys," he says calmly, "try not to strangle each other." He takes a sip of coffee, smacking his lips and letting out an "Ahhh." He's already spilled half the cup on his lap, but this doesn't bother him. Nothing does.

When we pull into the parking lot of Trollhaugen, the sight of the Cats grooming the shadowy hills brings butterflies to my stomach. My dad asks the ticket attendant if we can have a discount since all of us children are from an orphanage. We all groan with embarrassment. It's a line he uses every time we come here.

At Trollhaugen there's always polka music pumped through the loudspeaker. The sound of it means skiing and it sets off our adrenaline. We frantically push one another aside as we try to untie the knot of skis and poles, as if they will disappear if we don't grab them fast enough.

A big, burly farmer who works here during the off-season comes over to staple lift tickets to our jackets. His big sausage fingers are somehow unaffected by the cold. Though our jackets will never be the same after the staple is put in, we will wear our lift tickets proudly back to school, like tattoos.

Someday I dream of owning buckle boots and metal skis, but for now I lace my boots as tight as I can and ski on the long wooden planks I inherited from my brother. The tight spring-loaded bindings have enough built-up energy to launch a rocket. I have to have my brother stand on the front lever to get the bindings to close. They snap shut like a bear trap.

For a kid, the greatest difficulty of skiing is not the hill, but the tow rope. And today I will challenge myself by riding one of the fastest ropes in the area. In my eagerness, I grab the rope too tight and suddenly I go from zero to what seems like 30 before landing on my back. As I try to locate my legs and poles in the contorted pile I have become, the tow rope screams like a buzz saw inches from my face. I roll out of the track and shake the snow out of my gloves. The cold on my wrists makes my arms ache all the way to my shoulders.

I grab the rope again, but with icy mittens I can't get a grip. With the rope running through my hands, I begin to slide backward down the hill. Finally, the rope burns a groove into my mitten and I am able to regain my grip.

Now I am flying up the hill, my skis slapping the icy lift tracks like bobsleds. The top of the hill nears, but my pole bounces over the rope and becomes tangled. I can't let go! I fly past the unloading area and become airborne. The demonic rope lifts me off the ground by one arm, like a mother scolding a child in a grocery store. Finally I slip out of my mitten and crash to the ground. My mitten and ski pole miss the safety line and begin the return trip down the hill.

An attendant runs out of his warming house and trips the safety line. Instantly, the rope collapses and all the way down the hill, bodies of lift riders lie scattered because of me. My mitten still clings to the tow rope like a dismembered hand.

Going down the hill I hit some ice and skid out of control, and like a cornerback cutting down a halfback with an open field tackle, I take the legs out from beneath a large, bearded man. He goes down with a heavy thud and bellows a curse. His glasses come off so I don't think he sees me. I ski away from the scene of the crime as fast as I can. At the bottom of the hill I fall again, this time scattering people in the lift line.

But my skiing improves. Three times in the morning I make it all the way up and down the hill without falling. At noon I find my sister and head inside for lunch. When I step on the wooden floor of the chalet, I skid into the splits because there's a chunk of ice on the bottom of my boot.

Lunch is good because it's mostly sugar—Hostess cupcakes, pop and cocoa. By the time we finish eating, the snow in my pockets and socks has melted and I'm soaked. We stand by the fire to warm up before hitting the slopes again.

We attempt to ride the T-bar together. We do great until it's time to get off. We cross skis and collapse into a tangled, arguing heap. The attendant shuts off the lift and as he pulls us out of the way, we are still yelling at each other.

Later my dad skis by. "Hey, kids, check me out. Watch me waggle!" With skis locked together he performs the exotic quick turns he read about in some ski magazine. His baggy black ski pants snap in the breeze as he goes by.

At the end of the day I undo my icy laces, which are stiff as wire and step into tennis shoes. With the brief euphoria of ski boot removal, my shoes are feathers on my feet.

On the drive home, my dad leans forward trying to hear football on the radio. Lombardi's Packers flutter in and out of reception as we near the Minnesota border. With the game out of reach, my dad suggests we say the Rosary.

I wail in agony. How much stupid religion can we take in one day? My complaining earns me the assignment of leading the first Glorious Mystery. In protest I rattle off a Hail Mary in four seconds flat. Doesn't count. Too fast.

My dad catches my eye in the rearview mirror and for the first time all day, his tone is serious. Slow down and think about the words you're saying, he tells me. And don't forget to give thanks for the privilege of living in this country and being able to ski.

Absolutely Super America

The lifeless needle has collapsed. It lies in the red zone next to the E. The car needed gas two days ago but I just forgot. I got busy. Now I remember, on the freeway, at night, in the middle of winter. My heart pounds. I grip the wheel tighter and lean forward peering out into the darkness, looking for a station.

I tell myself E can't really mean Empty. Ford engineers must have built in an idiot factor for people like me. The red is meant to scare us, to move us to action. I turn off the radio as if this will improve mileage. I listen intently, fearing the dreaded sound of my engine coughing and wheezing on its own fumes.

I exit the freeway. Up ahead, the bright lights of a Food & Fuel. An oasis of fuel with twelve gas pumps! I'm a lost sailor who's found shore.

The station is flooded with light. The buzzing fluorescent bulbs give off a light as harsh as the reality of this off-the-freeway neighborhood. I get out and study the fueling options: Let's see, I can pay by cash inside or credit card out here. There's three different colored buttons for gas. There's gold for Premier and red for Ultratane. One's got detergent and another's got octane. I hope my car will forgive me for being cheap and choosing plain lead-free.

I squeeze the nozzle. Nothing. I squeeze again. Inside the store I see the clerks looking out at me. I don't want them to get on the loudspeaker to tell me what to do. I can figure it out. Again I review the instructions. Too late.

"Lift the lever on the pump then push the 'gas on' button," is squawked over the microphone. I wave a thank you, mortified in front of the other customers. I squeeze and the hose jolts to life and the pennies start ticking away with the rhythm of a train clicking rails. Digital lettering informs me that indeed, I am "FUELING."

I wash the winter-gray film from my windshield and headlights. Dirty black wiper fluid oozes from the squeegee and runs down the window like Tammy Faye's mascara. Looking for paper towels, I reach up into the empty dispenser. Two islands over, I find a towel dispenser packed so tightly, I mangle three dozen towels before I'm able to extract a whole sheet.

A car pulls in—a big boat of a car from the early '70s. A half-eaten Oldsmobile 88. A spark flies from a muffler as it hits the bump at the lot entrance. The car keeps rocking until it stops at the pump next to mine. The thump of muffled music from inside the car dies as the car is turned off, but the engine keeps chugging and kicking like a diesel until it finally sputters to a stop. A dog in the back seat explodes against the backseat window. With his bark he threatens to tear me apart just for looking in his direction.

A man opens the driver side door. The door whines from lack of grease. "Shaddup!!!" he says to the dog. A woman sits in the front seat and stares straight ahead, no expression on her face. Two children in the back seat with the dog watch me with big eyes. When I return a look in their direction, the dog bashes its nose on the window, and begins another round of barking. The man eyes me with suspicion, as if I'm trying to rile his pet.

The pump snaps off as the tank reaches its limit. I feel a need to pump gas until I hit an even dollar amount. This will be tough, however. I have 35 cents to go. I pump cautiously, creeping up into the nineties, penny by penny, the hose lurching with each stop and start until I hit $16.97.

I give it one last quick squeeze but the tank spits up fuel. I jump back to avoid getting gasoline on my shoes.

I go in to pay. I press in vain against a door that says E X I T an inch from my face. The clerk points to the other door and once again I smile a Forrest Gump–like thank you. Inside the store, teenagers hang out by the Slurpee machine, their tongues red from the cherry syrup of their drinks.

Standing in line, I look up at the four security monitors. Dark and shadowy figures pump their gas, while somber and silent customers wait in line to pay. The grainy video images make us all look like potential thieves or victims. It reminds me of what a trusting and personal place America has become.

The manager, "Scott," wears a short-sleeve shirt and a tie that lands a good three inches above his belt. He grabs the mike, and with the voice of Mission Control in Houston, he says, "Go ahead, pump four."

The cashier is quick and efficient and snaps her gum as she works. Without a smile or eye contact, she tells each customer to "Have a nice night now."

"What pump?" she asks me. I forgot to look.

"Umm, I'm the Ford out there," I stammer, pointing in the direction of my car. But a van now blocks the view.

43

With a sigh she checks the pump registers. "Sixteen ninety-seven," she says. As I write my check she rings up the man in the rusty Oldsmobile. He buys cigarettes, a Powerball ticket and three scratch-off game cards. He pays in cash, the last couple of dollars spilling onto the counter in nickels, dimes and quarters.

From inside my car I watch him walk out of the store. He stops to scratch the game cards. Nothing. He crumples the losing tickets and lets them fall to the ground. The Powerball ticket he tucks in his breast pocket. This is hope.

He opens the cranky car door, and the vehicle rocks as he settles in the driver seat. Without a word he starts the engine. Tonight he'll go home and watch the Powerball numbers come up on TV and maybe, just once, outrageous fortune will smile down upon him. The magic numbers will appear on the screen, and at last, everything in his life will be perfect.

March Badness

Shirts versus skins. Pick-up basketball. Eight of us—all late 30s or 40-somethings, lawyers, accountants, and other once-a-week athletes—make our way out to center court to negotiate the terms and conditions of our little four-on-four game. As we bend and stretch and tighten the laces of our high-tops, we pick teams like kids on a playground.

It's us against them. We're shirts. They're skins. Reluctantly, almost modestly, our opponents turn and peel off their T-shirts, wad them into little balls, and throw them off the court, sending them skidding over the wood floor to gym bags against the wall.

They turn around. It's the cast of The Full Monty. In all their middle-age glory, they strut their stuff back to mid-court, rubbing their bread-dough tummies, pulling up their shorts. It's not a pretty sight. Men with breasts. Between the four of them they carry a set of Michelin tires. But we on our side don't feel superior. But for the grace of our T-shirts go we.

The next ritual in our civilized war is deciding who guards whom. I haven't played basketball in years, so I'm a little nervous. I quickly choose my assignment. Like a lion picking the slowest and weakest of a herd of prey, I choose the least formidable of the group, a short guy who looks like a candidate for a pacemaker.

The game begins. My nervous energy turns to adrenaline. The first few trips up the floor I feel absolutely splendid. I congratulate myself for staying in shape by jogging. But as I soon discover, jogging to get in shape for basketball is like watching *People's Court* to get ready for the bar exam. Ten minutes into the game, I'm sucking wind, loafing up the court. Rebound opportunities become less interesting. I leave it to others to get back on defense.

Not only am I moving like a sedated Luc Longley, my basketball skills are as rusty as the fenders of a Pacer. My brain tells my body what to do, but my body doesn't listen. I attempt to drive through the lane, but the ball doesn't follow. I take a jump shot, and instead of the expected sweet sound of swish, there is nothing but deadly silence. My anemic shot falls short of everything, and dies in a whimpering dribble in the corner of the gym. My teammates look at one another wondering if that was a pass or shot.

The only thing that saves me is that the CPA I'm guarding looks like he's ready for CPR. His face, expressionless from exhaustion, is as pink as rare prime rib. Despite his fatigue, he courageously attempts a fast-break lay-up, but his feet get tangled up with one another. He goes down, suddenly and definitively, like a soldier felled on the battlefield. His wet body makes the sound of a giant squeegee on the cruel gym floor. His glasses skitter into the corner like a puck on ice. But he's okay, and the game continues.

Our first game is to 15, but neither team can sink the final bucket. Lay-ups are missed, bricks are launched. Finally, I get a wide-open shot from the free-throw line. My shot is comically long, but it accidentally bangs off the backboard into the basket. I try to keep a straight face as if I intended the bank shot. But everyone's too exhausted to give me a hard time. In celebration our team exchanges limp high-fives, before each of us goes off to a separate part of the gym walking in little circles, looking for oxygen.

It's hard to believe that this clumsy, earth-bound struggle of ours is the same game I've been watching on TV all winter—that slammin', jammin' airborne ballet. March Madness, the NBA and, of course, the Nike ads with the shadows, the light and, most importantly, the sweat. Michael Jordan, in slow motion, walks on air. All muscles and tendons. "Just do it," the commercial says.

So I did it, and I know I'll feel it for a week. I gather my stuff and get ready to leave. I'm the last one in the gym. Alone at the top of the key, I look up at the basket. I remember in high school I used to be able to touch the rim. Now, all these years later, I wonder what I've lost.

Just for kicks, I decide to give it a try. Dropping my bag, I run and jump. I am stunned and elated by the nick of the hard cold rim on my fingertip. How can this be? This is a miracle! I haven't lost a thing off my vertical jump in twenty-five years!

Triumphant, incredulous, I gather my bag and walk off the court, trying to figure out how it is that I have defeated time. "Let's see," I say to myself, "I have been watching what I eat; and there's that one leg machine at the club I use once in a while, and…"

Walking out the gym door, I remember one other thing that might account for this miracle. I look down at the swoosh logo on my high-tops. "Of course. The shoes." Just as I'm thinking I should be in a Nike ad, I stumble.

That's funny, I didn't notice that step coming

in. Turning around I see that it is not a step, but the floor itself. A brand new gym floor—a good four or five inches of material—has been laid directly over the old floor. Then, looking up at the baskets, it dawns on me: They haven't adjusted the height of the baskets to the new floor yet. The very thickness of the new floor represents the exact amount of vertical jump I've lost over the years.

The Nike song in my head ceases. My brief, euphoric fling with immortality ends with the realization that the younger, higher-jumping me is gone forever, covered over with a new me, like the old gym floor lying beneath the new one. In the end, gravity wins. You and me and even Michael, we all come back down to earth.

My Favorite Jock

I step onto the tennis court and observe my opponent readying himself for the match. He can't bend down to reach his feet, so instead of pulling his sweatpants off, he drops them into a pile around his ankles and half stumbles out of them.

Next, he fastens a corset around his back, puts braces on his wrists and wraps an Ace bandage around an elbow. Finally, he produces a metal knee brace. It isn't obvious which knee it's for—both are the size of cantaloupe and bear scars that look like laces on a football. I can't imagine which of the knees he considers good enough to not require a brace.

After all straps are secure, he shuffles hurriedly onto the court, a limping menagerie of sports injuries that date back to his college football days in the '30s. Through the years, the indefatigable jock has suffered more injuries, and had more operations, than I have had birthdays. Yet the old guy is so excited to play, he has forgotten to zip his shorts. I try to tell him but he waves me off, accusing me of stalling for time. He tells me to prepare to receive the thrashing of my life.

I decide to go real easy on him. I lob him a soft one over the net and he flubs it into the next court. I wonder if I'll be able to stay awake for the match.

A half hour later he's moving a little better. It's like playing against a backboard. He's shuffling (not running) back and forth retrieving everything.

"Hey, I'm getting loosened up! Watch my footwork. Am I gliding or what!" he says with sweat-soaked enthusiasm.

An hour later, the sun is beating down. I'm hot and ready to leave. I hit what I think is a sure-kill shot and am about to turn around, when, for one glorious moment, he actually kind of runs to the ball, digging it out miraculously for the point.

I suggest we call it a day on that high note. He looks at me like I've lost my mind. I've got to humor him. So we play on.

It's now getting to be almost two hours that we've played. I've had enough so I call him up to the net and tell him I'm finished.

"You big overfed sissy!" he says. "C'mon, for your old man. If my dad were alive, I'd do it for him." He's dripping sweat, leaving a puddle where he stands pleading his case. "Someday, when I'm long gone, you'll wish you played with me." How can I say no?

After nearly three hours, my mind is no longer on the game but on the silver-dollar-size blister on my right hand. My game has gone to hell and the old man is giddy with delight.

"I knew the pressure would get to you!" he yells.

In frustration I try to knock him over with the next shot. It hits the back fence—on the fly.

"I guess that's my game," he says, feigning a yawn. I no longer feel sorry for him.

I walk off the court and his taunts follow: "I knew my superior conditioning would pay off!" he exclaims as he reluctantly but triumphantly limps off the court.

"Hey kid, can we play tomorrow? Your old man is improving, isn't he? You saw me moving. I was a gazelle out there!"

***

That was the scene just a few years ago. But now, he's nearing 80 and has congestive heart failure. Sometimes he can barely get out of a chair without getting winded. An illustrious sports career that began during the Coolidge administration has finally come to an end—or so you'd think.

"I'm making a comeback!" he says. Despite his condition, he's still playing tennis and golf. But how does he manage with a heart condition?

"The heart," he explains, "is a highly overrated organ."

***

Today he calls me at the office to report on the miraculous new swing he's discovered on the driving range.

"I'm keeping my right elbow in, and I'm hitting the ball a mile," he says breathlessly, clearly intoxicated on a sports high. "I've never hit 'em better." For the hundredth time, he has found the secret to the perfect golf swing.

Tomorrow he will probably stay on the range hitting balls until dark. With each swing he'll believe he's getting a little bit better. And as fall disappears and winter approaches, he will be the last one on the range. A solitary figure, hitting off the frozen ground. It is only the falling snow that will force him from the tee for another winter of contemplating the season to come.

Thinking of my father and his awesome capacity for hope and optimism, I'm reminded of those last lines of *The Great Gatsby*: "tomorrow

we will run faster, stretch out our arms farther…
And one fine morning…"

And so, my favorite jock plays on, forever
moving into his prime.

Hard Times in Mexico

Time has come screeching to a complete standstill. I'm guessing it's about 10 p.m. but I have no way of telling for sure since they took my watch along with everything else before locking me up in this four-star Mexican correctional facility. There's nothing to mark the passage of time except the boozy and erratic breathing of my cellmate who lies passed out in the corner. I wish I were as drunk as he is so I could fall asleep and get through the night.

There is something foul and angry in the air. I'm not sure how much my cellmate is to be blamed, but as his backside is pointed menacingly in my direction, I move as far away from him as possible and settle down on the cold, dirty cement for the evening. There is no pillow, no blanket.

The night is turning chilly and all I have on are jeans and a short-sleeve shirt. I begin to shiver. A cockroach appears at my feet. I shoo it away and it scurries off with surprising speed and hides beneath my cellmate. I get up and start pacing the cell. Does anyone know where I am? How long will I be a prisoner? Will I miss my flight back home tomorrow?

I climb up to the window for a breath of air. There is a guard smoking outside. I'm tempted to ask him for a cigarette. I don't smoke but I've seen enough prison movies to know that when you're behind bars you're supposed to smoke. I return to my corner and think back on the events that led to my incarceration. I'm quite sure I'm the first person in history to end up in a Mexican jail while pursuing continuing legal education credits.

I am here in Cabo San Lucas with a group of lawyers. All week we've been attending seminars in the morning, then studying beach law in the afternoon. This being our last night in Mexico, a group of about eight of us went out to dinner. After dinner, we took a cab to a nightclub. Before we got in the cab, we negotiated a price with the driver. Upon our arrival at the nightclub, one of the lawyers in our party paid the driver, expecting about $10 in change. But the driver refused to return the change. The lawyer argued with the driver who eventually went and called somebody on his radio. Within minutes, three policia arrive.

None of the officers speaks English; so I, having mastered those Berlitz lessons on greetings and checking into a hotel, boldly step forward as interpreter.

The head officer orders us to pay the cab fare plus $7 for the cabbie's time. I explain that we have already paid the fare and are owed change. As I speak, I notice the two assistant officers, who have positioned themselves on either side of me, glaring and snarling like guard dogs waiting for the order to attack.

My explanation is met with a moment of silence that ends when the lead officer issues an order I don't understand. Suddenly, the two assistant officers each grab an arm and lead me to the squad car. One pushes my head down while the other pushes me into the back seat. The door slams shut. I look out at my shocked companions who look on helplessly. "What's going on?" I wonder. My Spanish is not the best. Did I inadvertently say something about one of their mothers?

The three policia get in the car with me. One of them joins me in the backseat of the car, with a rifle perched menacingly on his lap.

I lean over the front seat and ask the driver, "Adonde vamos?"

My seatmate jabs the barrel of the gun in my ribs and speaks the first English words I've heard from the group.

"Foke hew," he says as if spitting at me.

We wind through the streets and into the less populated outskirts. As the scene swirls past, I feel as if I'm in a bad dream. This can't be happening to me.

When we arrive at the jail, I am not charged with anything; I am just locked up. And now, here I sit. A strange, inconsequential thought occurs to me: I won't be able to brush or floss tonight.

Suddenly, I hear the sound of a liquid slapping the cement outside my cell. At first I think a pipe has burst. Then I see the source. The man in the cell across the hall is relieving himself through the bars of his cell. A puddle forms in the hallway, then snakes its way like the Rio Grande toward the drain in our cell.

When he finishes, he remains leaning against the bars. He groans at first, then bellows loudly at the guards.

"Tengo hambre!!!" When there's no response, he turns his drunken gaze in my direction. His bloodied lower lip is swollen to the size of a banana. He blinks me into focus and what he sees apparently makes him angry. He growls at me with disdain and yells something I can't understand. I pretend to ignore him, and the stream on the floor. He continues to scream at me. He's making my comatose cellmate look like inmate of the year.

Then the door opens. A guard hops over the puddle and unlocks my cell. I am led to the front desk where a couple of my lawyer friends—people I hardly knew six days ago—await. Apparently they had called the owner of the nightclub we were going to. The owner, having a financial interest in keeping tourists safe, made a call to the police and negotiated my release.

The guard tells me it will cost $40 to get out of jail. I gladly pay the bribe. I consider it a bargain.

I step out into the night with my friends, and the cool salty air feels like freedom itself. The past couple of hours have taught me a lot.

Back home now it seems everyone is complaining how screwed up our legal system is because some criminal got off on a technicality.

But we might take some solace in the fact that these confounding "technicalities" are evidence of a system that seeks to avoid at all cost incarcerating the innocent, even if it means letting the guilty go free on occasion.

For anyone lacking a full appreciation of the meaning of this core concept that lies at the heart of our system, just go almost anywhere outside the U.S. and try holding a cabbie to his word.

Rare Window

It's 9:15 and already I've got a big jump on the day. I'm halfway through the sports page, and after a couple of personal phone calls and the sharpening of pencils, I could conceivably be doing real work by 10:30.

But before I rush into anything, I need to get perspective—see the big picture. So I step to my office window and look down upon the passing human carnival that is Hennepin Avenue—the last bastion of good old-fashioned vice in our glass and steel city.

Across the street I see Mr. Businessman walking in a very businesslike way toward the adult bookstore. As one patron exits, he rushes for the open door as if he's catching an elevator.

In the parking lot behind the store is a man drunker than a groom at a stag party. He staggers to his feet, wobbles a moment and grins wildly, yelling something at somebody who's not there. He tries to take a step forward, but some invisible force—maybe the rotation of the earth—causes him to stumble backward like an outfielder who's badly misjudged a fly ball. He crashes into a dumpster and slithers to the ground. With his chin resting on his chest, he goes to sleep in the morning sun.

I work for a while, then get up and walk by the window—hold on, look who's coming out of the bookstore with his little brown bag of shame. Mr. Businessman scurries along the sidewalk like a cockroach when the lights come on. He's somebody's brother, father, son, or perhaps, somebody's boss. The fear of being seen turns the sunlight into his enemy.

In the parking lot, the cops have come to remove our friend from the dumpster. It looks like he is explaining to the officers how truly drunk he isn't. They move his dead-weight body into the waiting van like he's a Hefty bag full of kitchen trash.

Good show out my window this morning. Wow. It's noon already. Time for lunch.

****

I'm back from lunch, but I can't just dive right into work on a full stomach. It's kind of like not swimming after eating. So I step over to the window for a little peek at the start of the afternoon on the street of broken dreams.

A woman with huge hair, a micro mini-skirt and high heels that are an ankle fracture waiting to happen struts her way down Hennepin. She turns in to Augies Bar with its sign as old as the city, "TOPLESS GIRLS SHOW UNTIL 1 AM."

This woman is a blue-collar stripper who earns every worn dollar bill cast her way on stage. Did she ever dream as a little girl that it would come to this? Never mind. I have to work.

I meet with several key members of the editorial staff. Are we going to hyphenate "sky blue" on page 32 of the upcoming issue or aren't we? The pressure is intense—we have only two hours to decide. I listen to both sides of the argument. I show that I am deep in thought by rubbing my face with both hands and sighing heavily, the way Uncle Bill on *Family Affair* used to when trying to decide what to tell Mr. French to make Buffy and Jody for dinner.

I can't think sitting down so I move to the window for inspiration and insight. On the sidewalk I see two types of people: those who walk in straight lines because they are actually going someplace, and those lost souls who bounce from one random encounter to another trying to bum cigarettes, dope and change. If the percentage of straight-liners to wanderers is any indicia of the economic health of the state, we're in deep trouble.

Let's hyphenate, I decide. The staff hurries off to execute the hyphenation. I'm proud of my decisiveness but I am drained. I collapse in my chair and peel a banana.

Across the way on the rooftop of the 4th Street fire station I observe several firefighters setting up lawn chairs and applying suntan oil. If ever I find myself being rescued from a fire and smell coconut oil, I'll know why.

The afternoon sun pours into my office. I must have dozed off because the half-eaten banana is now in my lap. Got to wake up and work before calling it a day. And what better way to wake up than taking a short glance at Hennepin. It's nearly cocktail hour and a couple of middle-aged men, wearing loafers and crisply pressed jeans, walk with a tidy swagger from the Brass Rail to the Happy Hour Bar.

A couple of workers from our building hurry to their cars in the lot across the street making their way through the weaving drunks and past the slouched and bored unemployed who lean upon the railing that fronts the lot.

This has not been my most productive day.

Maybe it's because I have things on my mind. But what are my problems compared to those of the cast of characters on the street below? I turn from the window and call it a day. As I step outside into the fine spring evening, I am happy just to be walking in a straight line down Hennepin, with someplace to go.

September 1993

Gone Fishing

The clouds over Rainy Lake are dark and swollen and sagging lower by the minute. I'm in a boat with three high school friends about to embark on the camping trip we've been taking almost every summer since '77. As I look up at the threatening sky I am reminded of the weather map I saw in the morning paper; it showed a storm system the size of Iowa settling over the area. Nothing against my buddies, but the prospect of three days in a tent with them listening to the rain does not exactly thrill me.

Since we are on the Canadian side of Rainy, we need to stop off at Sid's cabin, as we do every year, and purchase our Canadian fishing licenses, camping permits and minnows. Sid lives alone in the middle of nowhere in this little cabin where we transact our business. It takes him forever to fill out the various forms; his thick brown fingers seem incapable of separating the various sheets of paper. Sid squints through the smoke of a filterless cigarette that clings to his moist lower lip, looking at each form as if it's the first time he's ever seen it. The harder he concentrates, the more his breathing sounds like a bulldog straining against a leash.

Sid finally finishes the paperwork and we follow him as he shuffles pigeon-toed down to the dock to fetch minnows out of the tank. As he bends down on all fours, his greasy blue jeans slip down, revealing more crack than a plumber.

Skimming dead minnows off the surface with his bear-paw hand, he offers them to us. "Them are free!" he says with a laugh before tossing them in the lake. After buying our minnows, we say good-bye to Sid and head off in search of our campsite and the great fish that lurk beneath these cold iron-tinted waters.

Miraculously, the rain holds off until after we set up camp. We are just starting to cook our burgers when the rain falls in sheets upon the island. We scramble for the tent while Rick heroically stays behind for the noble cause of cooked meat. But fighting the wind and cold rain, the butane fire beneath the pan provides little heat; the burgers don't really cook, but turn a listless gray.

When the rain subsides, the rest of us venture out of the tent for cocktail hour. Gary makes whiskey sevens so strong the ice never has a chance. When we finally crawl into our sleeping bags several highballs later, we are just this side of comatose. This is a good thing, for there is no hell on earth quite like lying sleepless in a tent, wedged shoulder to shoulder between three guys, listening to their snoring.

The next morning we awake and emerge from the tent to greet the cloudy new day. I can't figure out which is worse, my hangover or the fact I forgot to bring my now-soggy tennis shoes inside the tent after singing the Canadian National Anthem last night.

Nature is calling. With dread, I grab a roll of paper and begin my journey into the rain-soaked woods. As I walk I stir the brush, alerting billions of mosquitoes that a blood donor has arrived. In self-defense, I slap myself in a frenzy.

I emerge from the woods a new man. My beard is now grizzly and I am ready to go forth to kill what I must eat. We head out on the lake to fish for our next meal.

The sun appears later that morning and transforms the world. The shoreline lights up a brilliant green and the cold black water now turns a welcoming sky blue. By noon we are ready to take a swim and clean up. As I climb up the ladder onto the boat, Jim moons me from above just as he would have 20 years ago. He now has a family and an important job working for the Treasury Department in Washington, D.C. But it's somehow reassuring to know that behind the civilized façade lurks the soul of a high school sophomore.

Later that day the fishing is good, with Rick catching more than his share of walleyes. Suddenly Jim's rod bends like a horseshoe and the reel squeals as his line spins out. He's hooked something that feels like it's the size of a piano.

Gary cuts the engine and we all stare at the line in the water, wondering if what's at the end of it is animate or not. The line remains still in the water for a moment and then the answer comes. The line begins to move through the water with a mind all its own.

The rest of us stumble over each other, reaching for the net, grabbing the engine and looking for the camera. As the fish tires, Jim works frantically, cursing and shouting orders at us. As he brings the fish in, the reel groans against the great resistance.

We see the swirl of the water and finally, the long, dark green shadow of the monster northern pike. It looks to be well over fifteen pounds. The net is ready, the camera is rolling and the fish is still for a moment as it comes to the surface. Then suddenly there is a flash of white belly as it explodes through the surface and snaps its great head free.

It is a long, painful moment of silence. Jim stands with his limp line fluttering in the breeze wearing the expression of one who has just dropped his keys down a storm sewer. Considering the magnitude of the loss, Jim seems oddly composed. I'm thinking that maybe Jim has really matured and for a fleeting moment I feel sorry for him. Then, the eruption.

Every obscenity known to the English language rings out over the Canadian waters—each echo sounding like a lunatic from some distant shoreline. Jim rants and raves and curses at everything and everybody—the fish, the boat, the three of us. And for miles around us, his voice and our laughter are the only human sounds.

A Brief Journey

As we merge onto the interstate my mother's grip tightens on the steering wheel at ten and two o'clock. From the back seat I watch cars switch lanes and fly past us. We are a slow-moving oddity on the hurried freeway, out of the flow, like an Amish family in a buggy. I check over my mother's shoulder to see if maybe the car hasn't slipped into neutral.

My dad is in the passenger's seat. He looks smaller than my mother, the top of his head barely visible above the seat. He hasn't stopped talking since Minneapolis. I forget why, but he's naming the members of Franklin Roosevelt's third-term cabinet.

I try to shift position to regain feeling in my legs. I've been in the lotus position for the last fifty miles, sharing space in the back seat with a cooler, a pan of carrot cake, a garment bag and two suitcases. Though it's only a weekend trip, my parents have packed like Thurston and Lovey Howell. We've got enough clothes in the car for a substantial yard sale.

We are on our way to Chicago. My parents will stay with my sister and her husband, then I'm driving on to South Bend for a wedding. Had I made the trip alone, it would have been a six-and-a-half-hour trip to Chicago. As we pull over for our fifth stop, I'm not sure what day we will arrive.

I crawl from the wreckage of the back seat. Tumbling onto the sidewalk, my left leg remains in the back seat, tangled up in seat belts and baggage straps. I finally wrestle free. Like my parents, I limp with travel stiffness. The three of us squint in the afternoon sun, surveying the town of Menomonie, Wisconsin, looking for a place to eat.

There's a restaurant on the corner with plants and cappuccino and sprout-decked sandwiches. My dad vetoes this. Too clean. Too cutesy. We go next door.

Reading the menu on the door makes my face want to break out. The place is loud, smoky and greasy, just perfect for my dad.

There's a table of overgrown frat guys from

UW-Stout with tractor caps and chew waving an empty beer pitcher at their frizzy-haired blonde waitress. Though they're all in the same booth, they yell at each other loud enough to be heard across the street.

"Omigod you guys, I'm SOOO sure!" screams the waitress as she serves them. She bounces over to our table on cheerleader legs that look like they just got a fresh coat of varnish. As she greets us, I notice her bubble gum is the exact shade of her lipstick.

"What does the hamburger come with?" my dad asks. "Curly fries," she says. He can't hear her. Michael Bolton is screaming a refrain on the jukebox. He sounds like a man trying to pass a kidney stone. Two of the frat guys have begun to arm wrestle. My dad is baffled. "What are girly fries?" he wonders. My parents look small behind their menus as curly fries are explained to them.

Just as our meal arrives, a guy begins a game of pinball beside our table. He takes a hit off his Marlboro then leans over and begins his frantic play. His rear hovers over our table. Each jerk and twitch of his body produces a series of brain-damaging dings and buzzes.

After about five minutes of this, I realize I'm unable to derive maximum enjoyment from my curly fries. My dad, who has spilled a good deal of mustard on his shirt, is greatly amused by my exasperation. Picking up my silverware, I realize that the pinball wizard's dirty Levi's are within a fork jab from my face. I'm tempted, but I choose the civilized approach and ask Mr. Brain-dead if he can finish his game after we're done eating. He grunts and sulks away from the game. My mother is relieved her son is not being thrown over a pinball machine. My dad laughs to himself, delighted with the greasy, raucous life of the place.

We make it to my sister's and the next day I drive on to South Bend. Indiana is a week or two ahead of us in Minnesota. While everything is still brown back home, here, every limb of every tree is swollen with blossoms.

The wedding is beautiful and at a post-reception party, I'm cornered by somebody's Uncle Jack. Jack is a veteran postal worker who has enough alcohol in him to cause a small explosion. When he finds out I'm in the magazine business, he bobs and weaves like a fighter who's been tagged with a solid uppercut. His bloodshot eyes come nowhere close to focusing on me as he swears to almighty God he can save me thousands on my postage.

"Really?" I say. Apparently my voice does not register enough sincerity. "You think I'm shittin' you?" he spews. "I ain't shittin' you, man.

Thousands. I could save you thousands!" He drops his beer and is the only one in the place that doesn't notice.

On the drive back to Minneapolis my dad's chatter continues. He is reminiscing about the great Gopher football teams of the '30s and '40s. "There was Bud Wilkinson, Babe LeVoir... Pug Lund..." His speech slows and his head bobs, "Sonny Franck and...Leo Nomellini and... Bruce..." And just like that, he drifts off, sound asleep.

In the momentary silence, out of nowhere, I think of a friend who's sick with cancer. I've got to visit or call her. I check my Day Timer. I still have Kelly's number at the hospital. I make a note on my to-do list to call her when I get home.

***

The answering machine is blinking frantically when I walk in the door of my apartment. The last of the messages is from a friend of Kelly's whose voice shakes unnaturally. I don't need to listen to know the message. Still in her twenties, Kelly is gone, just like that. She died this morning.

The wind through the windows smells like rain and I jump when a door in another room slams. I step out to the deck and watch the coming storm. In the distance I hear a downpour but below the sidewalk is still dry white. One by one at first, then in a collective applause, big drops of rain splatter like giant tears leaving the sidewalk a spotted brown. I watch until the dots connect, then go inside.

Who can make sense of this? It seems we are all tops spinning: each wobble a wrinkle, a birthday or a creak of the joint. Eventually we all wind down and fall. For some it's sudden and in youth; for others it's gradual, but it always seems to happen too soon.

Home for Christmas

It's a bad hair day on the fourth floor of the Moose Lake Treatment Center. Though it's past three in the afternoon, it doesn't look like anybody's had a chance to shower yet today. But what's the rush? Nobody's going anywhere anyhow.

I walk into the lounge to see if my friend Bob is there. A patient in a flannel shirt whose dirty socks have grown long in the toes rocks back and forth in front of the TV, hugging his stomach and mumbling to himself. With his sleep-formed hair he looks like Lyle Lovett the morning after.

Then I spot him. The kid who was my best friend in grade school is now the slightly stooped, bearded man pacing in circles at the end of the hall. As I walk down the dark, tiled hallway, I prepare my words of apology. I haven't visited him in nearly a year because ever since he was moved up here to Moose Lake, I've convinced myself I didn't have the time to make the two-hour drive from the Cities to see him.

I am now only a few feet away from him and he hasn't looked at me. Just as I am about to speak, he says, as if he's continuing a conversation we had over breakfast, "So, White, is your mother okay? I heard she had an operation."

I stumble for a moment. "Um, well, she's doing great, Bob. Thanks for asking. But how are you doing?"

Even though it's a raw December day and we're north of Hinckley, Bob's dressed like he's on a cruise. He's in a short-sleeve shirt, Bermuda shorts, loafers and no socks. He bends to touch his toes and holds the position for a good twenty seconds. It's difficult to converse while his head is near the floor, so I wait.

Then he stands up abruptly as if he just remembered something terribly important from the seventh grade. "You remember the time Miss Muvich threw you against the lockers?" He laughs the same laugh he had in school. "White. You're such a troublemaker!"

As we walk toward the visitor's lounge Bob tells me he's been reading a book for the past three months. He stops in his tracks and stares at the ceiling, his brow creased with the effort of trying to remember the precise page he's on. "I think it's page one…thirty…four."

Inexplicably, he steps out of his loafers and continues walking down the hall. "Bob, your shoes, maybe…"

He smothers my words as he confides, "I don't tell a lot of people this, but (lowering his voice) sometimes I use a ruler to guide my eyes down the page."

"Well, that's great, Bob, but why don't you want anyone to know?"

He's surprised that I would ask such a stupid question. "C'mon, White. You know how competitive reading is! You just don't go around telling everybody your secrets to reading, do you?"

"Yeah, that's true, Bob, I guess I don't." I look back at the vacant loafers in the middle of the hall, positioned at the very angle his feet stood. They look as though the former occupant vanished into thin air.

In grade school everybody liked Bob. He was funny and smart and always in trouble with the nuns. He was also a gifted kid who could sing and play guitar, and was the best artist in the class. As an athlete, he was the kind of player that would dive over bushes to catch a fly ball and emerge with a grass stain on his shoulder and the ball in his glove.

He was, and remains, a humble, unassuming guy who is an unfailingly loyal friend.

I lost track of him after high school. He earned a degree from the university, and then the gradual decline began. No accident. No drugs. Nobody's fault, just a glitch in the software of the mind—one of those things that could happen to any of us.

I bumped into him again years after high school. He was playing guitar in the skyways and working as a janitor. He seemed a little spacey, but I figured he was just a starving artist who was smoking a little too much pot, or something.

It wasn't until I had lunch with him a couple of years later that I realized something else was going on. When the waitress asked for his order, his eyes widened in panic and confusion. Like an ill-prepared student guessing on a multiple choice exam, he blurted out random items off the menu: milk, soup, pancakes, Coke. I finally had to order for him. It was at that meal that he informed me he was having trouble organizing his thoughts and was taking medication for the problem.

Up until four years ago, we used to play golf. In one of the great mysteries of nature, it seemed that as his illness got worse, his game improved. Though he would go an entire round without being able to tie his shoes, he could shoot in the 70's.

Finally, it just took too long for him to play.

He'd hit a spectacular iron shot within feet of the pin, but instead of walking to his ball, he'd sit down on the fairway to reorganize the contents of his bag.

Now we sit in the lounge and watch the Lions and Packers on TV. I am grateful for the distraction of football. In the corner stands a Christmas tree with tinseled decorations that say "Merry Christmas!" But in this locked facility, these words seem as void of joy as a forced smile.

But Bob is not depressed. He tells me he thinks he'll have a better shot at getting a job once he shaves his beard. I tell him I don't think his beard will hurt his professional chances one bit. He stands up and once again bends down to touch his toes.

As I watch his shirt fall down over his face I realize there is no way to sugarcoat the loss. Bob might never go home again. But maybe, somehow, this cross he's been given is a ticket to salvation if he chooses. Then I realize his butt is still in my face and I have to laugh. He stands up, and doing a perfect Miss Muvich impersonation, he accuses me of being a troublemaker, and laughs along with me.

Bitten in the Garden

N eighbors slow down and frown as they drive past my yard. They survey the meadow that is supposed to be my lawn. They don't know it, but I can read their lips as they form the words "garbage house" and "dump." Frankly, this hurts.

First of all, I'm not into gardening or lawn care. If I had my way, I'd AstroTurf the whole thing and be done with it.

Second, what do people expect of me anyhow? I just moved in (six months ago) and haven't had a chance to get a lawn mower. Besides, who has time for yard work? These people have no idea how time consuming eighteen holes of golf can be, especially when you throw in cocktails afterward. It's a miracle I have time to stop by the office, let alone tend to the yard.

But enough's enough. The grass is lying on its side and I suppose I'm in danger of a misdemeanor lawn violation. It's time to invest in some quality lawn equipment. I open the Yellow Pages to Used Mowers. Here we go, Dick's Used Mowers.

My car scrapes the driveway as I turn in to Dick's, which is located in a very rough part of town. Dick himself is a walking oil change. No amount of Lava soap could ever remove the years of engine grease from this man's hands. Never once does he remove the cigarette from his lips as he shows me his fleet of used and reconditioned Toros and Lawn-Boys. I'm attracted to the modest price tag of an older Toro.

"'64 was a very good year for Toro," Dick says, squinting through the cigarette smoke. "Go ahead, give 'er a try."

After a couple of pulls, the machine sputters to life, then roars. Dick smiles like a proud father as the mower spits sand and pebbles across the asphalt. I'm so pleased I don't even haggle on the price. "Do you have change for a $20?"

As I load the old Toro in the trunk, I ask Dick what kind of return policy he has.

He laughs as if I'm kidding. "It's sold 'as is.' Once you leave the parking lot, I've never seen you or the mower in my life," he says as he moves on to help another customer.

Fair enough. Just thought I'd ask. As I head

home with my trunk lid bobbing in the rearview mirror, I'm getting kind of excited about mowing my own lawn.

Once in the tall grass, however, the Toro loses its will to live. The engine sounds anemic and the blade revolves slower than a ceiling fan. The tired old Toro can only bend the grass. Call me picky, but I was kind of hoping for a mower that could actually cut the grass.

In the middle of the yard, the machine sputters and gasps and finally chugs to a halt. I try to make some adjustments to the engine with a series of drop kicks. I pull the starter cord forty or fifty times, each time mumbling to myself what I think Dick ought to do with his Toros and Lawn-Boys.

Fortunately, my neighbor comes to my rescue and loans me his mower. Finally, I get the lawn mowed, and for the first time since I bought the house, the yard actually looks decent.

After returning the mower to my neighbor, I stop and look with pride upon my property. But I now see imperfections I hadn't noticed before. There's that overgrown dogwood bush with its gnarled limbs. Like a giant arthritic hand it claws and scratches the side of the house every time the wind blows. It has aspirations of becoming a tree, and unless I do something, I'll have a limb growing into the dining room soon.

Being short of tools, I grab a serrated bread knife from the kitchen. The angry bush attempts to put my eye out as I crawl to its base. Lying on my stomach, with branches down my shirt and in my hair, I begin sawing. An hour later, the great bush topples.

The carcass is the size of a minivan. As I drag it to the driveway I have a sense of accomplishment and pride, like I just bagged a deer. I'm sort of into this yard thing now.

I notice a flower box in front. Wouldn't it be nice to have some flowers? I've never grown a flower in my life. Perhaps tomorrow I'll visit the nursery.

I buy too many flowers for the window box, which necessitates the planting of flowers in the ground, which leads to the purchase of a shovel and peat moss and manure.

I dig a garden. Then another. I make repeated trips to the nursery, racking up a bill like a gambling debt. I can't stop planting. I plant vegetables I don't know how to eat—kale, Swiss chard. I plant flowers I've never heard of. I develop a terrible Miracle-Gro habit. I gotta have the terra cotta pots.

A couple of months later, I've got a produce department in my back yard. I could pour a jar of salad dressing on the garden and I'd have dinner.

Anyone coming within 50 yards of my property is subjected to the same tour. I have the speech memorized. I tell them about the miracle of the dogwood, which has come back as a beautifully shaped bush. I show them the zinnias I planted from seed and the watermelon I transplanted from a friend's garden. But the highlight of the tour is the compost pile with its banana peels and grass clippings.

By this time, people are generally cross-eyed with boredom. But that's okay. Next year's garden will dazzle them. I have great plans for next year. I can't wait for the first chance in spring to dig in the garden, turn the cool earth, and create something better.

Gone to California

E verywhere you look, it's like a picture off a wine label—the rolling hills, the vines heavy with grapes ready for picking. It's 10 a.m. and most of our party has a happy-hour buzz. We are in Napa Valley at the Joseph Phelps winery, and our tour guide has his nose in a glass of Merlot. If he inhales any harder, he could take the liquid up the schnoz like a Shop-Vac.

"This is truly an amazing wine," he says. He takes a sip and smacks his lips. With his hand holding only the edge of the base of the glass, he twirls the glass with amazing dexterity, the wine spinning like it's in a blender. I try to do the same, but it's like doing the hula-hoop. I can't get the centrifugal action going. A wave of wine leaps from my glass. I've got this truly amazing

Merlot on my shoes.

The next wine he describes has all the at-
tributes that someday I'd like to see in myself.
It's bold, well-balanced, straightforward, and
yes, honest. Even though I don't know Chablis
from Shinola, the adjectives I'm picking up on
this trip will help me fake my way through any
dinner party.

"This wine," he says, as he fills our glasses
with a Chardonnay, "is a little buttery." The food
product analogies are flying rampant around wine
country these days. Last night our waiter sug-
gested a wine that he said is "almost coconutty." If
I want coconut, I'll order a piña colada. Whatever. I
swirl the wine. People around me run for cover.

"Can you feel the seamlessness of the wine?
There are no gaps in this wine. That's what's so
remarkable." Hmmm. No gaps in the wine. I
make a note of this. I can't wait to get home and
rant in a restaurant. "Waiter, there's a gap in my
wine!!!"

After a few days in wine country, seven of
us pile into a rented car and drive down to San
Francisco, each of us sitting on one cheek the
whole journey. When we arrive in the city, three of
us have maps out at the same time. We simultaneously give the driver different directions. Wisely,
he ignores all of us.

Slowly and tentatively, we navigate the boat

through the crowded streets. We go up a hill so steep the blood shifts as our feet rise above our heads. We lie on our backs like astronauts on a launching pad, waiting for the light to turn green. I look out the back window. Brake failure here could land us in the Pacific.

We finally make it to our hotel near Union Square. After checking in, we decide to go on a walking tour of the city. One step out of the lobby and we are approached. A sad-looking kid, his face self-mutilated with nose and lip piercings, mumbles that he needs some change. Behind him, a cable car stops in the street. It is overflowing with happy tourists who cling to it like refugees to a lifeboat. With their cameras and purses and sunglasses, they are large children waiting for the ride at the fair to start up again.

A half block down, at the corner of Powell and Geary, is the St. Francis Hotel with its grand lobby, one of the finest hotels in America. In Dewey's, the dark paneled bar off the St. Francis lobby, businessmen confer in low tones over brandy and cigars. Outside, a man whose face is dirty as a coal miner sits on the sidewalk, his legs sprawled in front of him, a cat on his lap. His icy blue eyes are lifeless. He doesn't bother to look up to ask for money. In this competitive marketplace of street people, he doesn't stand a chance. His hat has only a couple of coins.

Coming down the street is the real pro. He walks stride for stride next to the tourists singing "Ain't Too Proud to Beg," in a voice that is, well, buttery and seamless. The tourists can't help but smile. "Yo, can y'all do me a favor?" he says. "If my song brought you a little joy, could y'all hep me out wissome spare change? God bless y'all." He pockets the money and turns to pursue his next target.

The birthplace of the peace movement is an ordinary intersection. At Haight and Ashbury, there's now a Gap on one corner, a Ben & Jerry's on the other. Down the street, at the edge of Golden Gate Park, it's a shopping cart convention. Leftover flower children, now toothless and gray, mumble to themselves and pick through trash cans, filling the bulging black plastic bags they tie to their carts.

In the center of the park, aristocratic and hunched-back seniors are decked out in white. On a giant lawn, smooth and short as a putting green, they are lawn bowling. With skinny brown arms, and shaky determination, they roll the heavy black balls. Despite the feeble starts, the balls continue to roll, slow and smooth, like pool balls over felt.

We go deeper into the park. It's nearly midday and there are some who are just now rising from their sleeping bags and blankets. A bearded

Manson look-alike scratches himself and lights the day's first cigarette.

***

I grew up hearing stories about San Francisco from my mother. How my grandfather watched the city burn after the earthquake of 1906, how she remembers the building of the Golden Gate Bridge. And when she talks about San Francisco during the war, you half expect to hear Glenn Miller strike up the band. In those years, it was a city of sad good-byes.

More than a half century ago, she stood on the pier and waved good-bye to a soldier on the deck of a ship headed off to war. As the ship pulled away, the soldier frantically scribbled love notes, tied them to stones and threw them to her. She gathered up the notes, and through her tears read them, wondering if she'd ever see him again. It seems so corny to us now, like something out of a Frank Capra movie. She still has the notes my dad wrote that day, but the city she remembers no longer remains.

Today I walk by a newsstand. The headlines of the *Chronicle* tell us that O.J. is playing golf again; Farrakhan says women aren't invited; McVeigh was not alone. We are a splintered nation, suspicious of each other—a country, it seems, on the verge of war with itself. As we walk out of our hotel for the airport, for the 50th time in two days, a hand reaches out. "Spare change?" I don't know what to say.

Dome and Dumber

Roy and I sit in the back seat of his dad's car. Beneath my parka, I wear the complete contents of my sweater drawer and I'm boiling hot. Looking out at the bright sunshine it's hard to believe it's as cold as the radio says it is. But upon closer inspection, you can see the evidence of the cold: the wisps of exhaust snapping and spinning out of the tail pipe of the car in front of us, and the black ice on the street formed from frozen exhaust.

In my hand, I study the precious ticket: "Admit one. Cleveland Browns at Minnesota Vikings. 1969 NFL Championship Game." The glossy ticket smells good, like a new magazine.

Roy and I are lucky to have these tickets. Six adults, acting foolishly by being sensible, passed on the opportunity to sit in the arctic cold of Metropolitan Stadium to watch this all-important playoff matchup. But Roy and I, devoted adolescent fans, would give up a foot to frostbite to see this game.

My heartbeat quickens as the erector-set stadium comes into view. Men in orange vests wave us into the parking lot and grimace against the cold. As we turn in to our parking space, the tires whine and squeak on the hard-packed snow.

Clutching old black and red checkered blankets to sit on, Roy and I follow his dad as he searches the parking lot for his friend's tailgate party. Our eyes water from the cold, and after a short while we have to walk backwards against the wind.

We find the party. It's a loud group of big round men in snowmobile suits. Huddled around two barbecue grills, they look like a group of penguins as they shift from foot to foot.

The host greets us with eyes red and happy with drink. His nose is as purple as the Vikings stocking cap upon his head, and from the nose little capillaries crawl out across his face like the back roads on a map. He offers Roy and me a hot cup of cider from a scotch-plaid thermos. "Boys, it's the only thing we have around here that doesn't have booze in it!!!" he roars as he hands us the steaming cups. He lights a Viceroy and howls, "Go Vikes!!!" to no one in particular.

After the party we head into the stadium. Our seats in the upper deck are unprotected from the brutal wind. But the sheer excitement of being here makes us forget about the weather. Down on the field, Bill Brown, the buzz-cut Viking fullback plays in bare arms and hands, and the stoic figure of Bud Grant stands like a granite monument upon the distant sideline.

The teams line up at the line of scrimmage, snorting big clouds of exhaust. And when Joe Kapp throws a long scoring strike, the play produces a muffled thunder as 48,000 fans clap their mittens and stomp their cold feet.

At halftime I head to the men's room and wait in a line that is ten deep. A heater mounted in the corner blows down upon us. When the time comes for me to step up to the trough, I begin the fumbling search—unzipping and unbuttoning through layers of clothing.

I stand there staring into the trough, acutely aware of the dozen men behind me, whose beer-swollen bladders wait anxiously for me to finish. But nothing happens. Stage fright has the best of me. As I concentrate in vane, a cigarette floats past. What do I do? I can't just turn around and leave. But I can't stand here all day either. Finally, like the first drops of a long-awaited rain, it begins. I stare at the ceiling in relief, and listen to the men talk of football.

As the fourth quarter winds down, the Vikings are just minutes from a Super Bowl. We promise Roy's dad we'll meet him back at the car and run off before he can object. We dart through the crowd, down to the field. We wait for the right moment, then jump the fence and run past the slow and half-hearted security guards. Soon, the sidelines are encircled by fans. We stand next to the end zone and watch my hero, Joe Kapp, who is just a dozen yards away, as he brings the massive Vikings to the line of scrimmage. The stadium lights have come on now as the final seconds of football in this decade tick away.

The gun sounds and it's official: the Vikings are going to the Super Bowl! Roy and I join the stampede of fans running onto the field. As Joe Kapp heads for the sideline, I leap up and slap his shoulder pad. As the goal posts are pulled down by jubilant fans, Roy and I stand in the center of the field. We have to turn our shoulders to look at each other through our fur-lined hoods. We laugh in disbelief. I take off my mittens and bend down to touch the sacred, frozen ground. And looking up into the emptying stands, I vow I will never forget this moment.

***

Twenty-five years later I'm offered four tickets to the Vikings. These are good seats that might go to waste if I don't take them. I have better things to do, but I think about the good-uncle points I might rack up if I take my 10-year-old nephew, Kyle. So I invite him, my brother-in-law and a friend to the game.

It's cold outside. But inside the living room comfort of the Dome, the men wear Dockers and loafers and cardigan sweaters. On the synthetic surface below, our millionaires play their millionaires. The spiritless game is interrupted by long, unnatural time-outs so that commercials can be played for the much larger, and more important, television audience.

Sipping a flat, over-priced beer, I'm a lethargic fan, as complacent as a husband in a La-Z-Boy. I don't even need to watch the game—if I miss something I can watch the replay on the scoreboard. Instead of football, we talk about computers and movies. Then I begin to pontificate on the ruined state of sports, on the dumbness of the Dome and on the way Viking football used to be—and the way it ought to be. Kyle ignores the foolish talk of the grownups, and instead, with wide-eyed wonder, he watches his heroes play the game.

Movers and Shakers

What a deal. The hide-a-bed sofa is in good shape. And it's mine if I want it. "Are you sure you don't want anything for it?" I ask my friends, Keith and Cindy.

"No, please. Take it. It's yours," they insist. There's almost desperation in their voices.

No problem. My buddy Tom has a pick-up truck, and between the two of us, no piece of furniture is too heavy. Like a couple of morticians who've come to take the body, we show up at Keith and Cindy's house just as dinner's being served. "Hey, ham, that smells good," Tom says as we track through the kitchen. Like a dog sniffing for scraps, he hovers near the stove. Cindy steers us out of the kitchen, and directs us to the sofa. Upstairs.

The couch seems designed to prevent easy lifting. All corners are rounded so there is nothing to grab on to. I need to pry my fingers underneath it to get a grip. Like a Soviet weightlifter I squat down low, my knees even with my ears, determined to get under the lift and not hurt myself.

I am eye level with Tom, who's at the other end of the sofa, his face peeking over the armrest. "Ready?" I ask. We haven't lifted yet and already the vein in Tom's forehead is showing.

"All right. Lift!!!"

Slowly we rise. The couch feels as if it's loaded with car batteries. The carpet where the couch was is as flat as cement. Tom starts panting like he's about to go into labor.

We shuffle across the room, a rapid duck walk, our butts out. Breathing hard, we can't speak in full sentences. Phrases come out in huffy one-word bursts. "Watchit. Thatsit. Lookout! Holdit. Dammit Tom! Gotit? Ohshit. Wait-a-sec!"

We set the couch down. Tom and I catch our breath, and curse the weight of the beast. "Sonnofah" we gasp. We can't finish the words. I'm beginning to understand why even charities won't come and haul a hide-a-bed. Hide-a-beds are like fruitcakes—big heavy things people are dying to get rid of.

We lift again and proceed down the hallway. Pictures fall off the wall, corners are dented, and woodwork is gouged. With each collision, Tom and I simultaneously blame each other. Behind us is a wake of destruction. As we make our way down the hallway, the resale value of the home continues to drop.

We pause at the top of the stairs. There's a landing and a turn. We vaguely discuss our strategy. Before I'm sure of what our plan is, Tom's lifting the couch, I'm on the bottom.

With my face smashed up against the side of the couch, I tap around behind me with my foot looking for the next step down. My nose begins to itch. My back quivers with strain. With each step down, the couch gets heavier. Rather than lifting, it feels like Tom is lying on the couch.

I think I've reached the landing but I've miscalculated. I stumble and land against the wall, pinned by the couch, which now feels heavy as a piano against my sternum. Apparently Tom has gone to play tennis or something, because there's no sign of help coming. Finally, I hear him say, "Hey, man, what the hell you doing back there?" If I were Moe and he were Curly, this is the part where I poke him in the eyes.

On the landing we tip the couch on its end and flip it over to turn the corner. It is here on the narrow stairway that the couch demonstrates its hide-a-bed feature. The mattress pops out like a jack-in-the-box, the heavy springs groaning as the bed unfolds. Nickels and Fritos and toys tumble out with the mattress. I bend down to pick up a rattle off the floor. As I try to straighten, it is then that I realize that I will probably never stand upright again. That's okay. Maybe I can get a job ringing bells at a church someplace.

We finally make it to my house. I remove the front door to make room for the sofa. It's a very tight squeeze. Tom and I push the sofa as hard as we can. Unfortunately, the sofa is wider in the middle. Our efforts only wedge the piece tighter in the doorway. The sofa is stuck. There is no moving it. The house creaks as it adjusts to the new permanent addition.

I try to look on the bright side. Perhaps the hide-a-bed in the front door will help deter burglars. Maybe it will give my home a distinctive look. Oh sure, a sofa stuck in the doorway may decrease the resale value of my home. But on the other hand, the hide-a-bed is bound to have gone up in value, now that it comes with a home.

Walk the Dog

Through clenched teeth I read: "Penn 4." His breath hot and panting, around the green tennis ball set deep in his mouth. He surrenders the soggy ball, which drops to the floor with a wet, bounceless thud. A gift from him to me.

I cannot insult him. With two fingers I lift the gooey ball, and for the 38th time today, I toss the ball across the room. He runs over the Sunday paper, scattering Target ads. On the hardwood floor he skids and just before smashing his head on the dining room table, he snaps up the ball in mid-bounce. He brings it back, panting, waiting, eternally ready for more.

I'm dog-sitting the three-year-old Newfie-Lab my girlfriend adopted last week. Linda warned me he likes to play fetch. I thought maybe I could get some work done while I watch him. But I don't think this will be possible. Okay, it's time for me to move.

At the closet, I grab my jacket and look at him. His breathing stops. He watches me. Like the accused, he stands before me, waiting for the verdict—tense, pleading, hopeful. Can he come with? Or will he be left, sentenced to a cruel and indefinite term of solitary confinement? He tilts his head.

"Wanna go for a walk?" I whisper.

His legs buckle with joy. He jumps and spins. Down the stairs he runs. Then back upstairs to me, hyperventilating. "Do I wanna go for a walk? What, are you kidding?"

He's won the dog lottery. One of the greatest things that could possibly ever happen in a dog's life is about to happen. He's going for a w-a-l-k.

I search room to room for my keys and he's with me every step of the way, offering to help. His big tail bangs a drum solo through the house. "Wack. Wack. Thump." The coffee table, the wall, the door. "Ping," it hits the metal leg of the kitchen table.

As I walk down the hall, he's in front of me, tongue out, back-peddling, too big and too excited to figure out how to turn around in the confined space and walk forward.

I grab his leash and put a hand on the doorknob. His nose at the crack of the door twitches with the scent of the cold air that seeps in. I pull the door open, bopping his snout. If he were a human there'd be cussing and tears and perhaps a bloody nose. But he's a dog. Nothing hurts. Besides, he's too excited, too grateful to notice.

He pulls with the strength of a sled dog. I'm the one being taken for a walk. And it's faster than a walk. I lean back against the straining leash, taking giant, loping strides. He's on an urgent mission, zigzagging from scent to scent, his tail waving like a windshield wiper set on high.

He stops. Sniffs. Unimpressed, he lifts a leg. The snow sufficiently yellowed, he hops on one leg as he finishes and moves from the scene. We continue the stop-and-go journey. A tree, a bush, the light post. Pit stops, sales calls. He leaves his card at each location.

A neighbor I hardly know rushes down her sidewalk. But it's not me she greets. "Oh, look at you! Aren't you a handsome pooch. Yessss you are," she says in baby-talk. Grabbing the dog's jowls, she asks, "What's your name, fella, huh? Wuzzz your name?"

I stand there, non-entity, leash holder, a mouthpiece for a dog. "Chester," I respond, not sure if I'm being rude by interrupting her conversation with the dog.

Chester's muzzle disappears up her jacket.

"My, aren't you a friendly boy," she says, attempting to repel him. But he's insistent, sniffing and snorting like an addict. Ms. Manners would not approve. I pull him away, apologizing. She says good-bye to him. His tongue dangles lecherously. We continue our journey.

Suddenly, out of nowhere comes a Doberman without a leash. He descends upon us like a border patrol. He wants to check passports. Open luggage.

Chester thinks it's playtime. His tail wags. He jumps playfully. But the Doberman has no sense of humor. I'm a little nervous. The muscular Doberman looks uptight. If a fight broke out between these two it would be Mike Tyson vs. Gomer Pyle. I pull Chester from the scene. Fortunately, the Doberman lets us off with a warning.

Down the street, he finds sacred ground. He sniffs, he circles. He's set. With hunched shoulder he looks around. Guilty. Embarrassed. He shakes and shudders. Steam rises from the snow bank. He steps away, scratching the snow with his paw like a batter stepping up to the plate, a half-hearted attempt to cover up his work.

I move in for clean-up duty. Baggy turned inside out over both hands, I encircle the area, excavating a buffer zone of snow around the pile. At a crucial moment in this delicate procedure, he sees something across the street. The leash strapped to my left wrist is snapped with a violent jerk and the contents of the bag go airborne. It's on my gloves and jacket. I curse the canine but find it impossible to stay mad at this good-natured animal.

At home he walks across the linoleum floor to his water bowl. Click, click, click. Lop, lop, lop, lop. He steps away from the bowl, still licking his lips, water dribbling down his chin. Like a night watchman, he makes his rounds, checks the windows for squirrels and trespassers. Everything's in order. He can relax. With a sigh, he drops in a heap, his chin resting on the floor. He snorts. When I talk to him, his forehead furls as he looks up at me. He rolls over on his side, and within minutes, his paws twitch as he sleeps. In his dog dreams, he catches a Frisbee on a beach.

I need to run to the store real quick. This time I tell him to stay. It kills him to obey, but he does. As I lock the door, I see him standing there. Through the glass I explain that I'll be right back. But he doesn't understand. For a dog, each good-bye could be forever. And each arrival is a miraculous homecoming. The heartbreak. The elation. While I'm away he'll plant himself on the middle of my bed, and plan the rest of his day. It's all in a day in the life of a dog.

The Journey of 1969

On the map, it looks simple. Our house is here in Minneapolis. We go out the driveway, scoot over to South Dakota, then down through Nebraska, Colorado, to Arizona. We walk to the bottom of the Grand Canyon and then drive home. While we're down there, we might as well swing through New Mexico, Texas, Oklahoma, Kansas and Iowa. Simple. Eleven states in ten days. Oh, and one other thing: we camp out the whole way.

With six kids in the family, my dad packs us off in twos to go on these epic summer journeys. My brothers, Jim and Bob, went together a few years back. They haven't spoken since. Now it's my turn to go. I'm teamed with my older sister, Jean. Jean doesn't want to go. She sits in the back seat staring straight ahead like she's serving detention. My dad thinks the adventure will be great fun. He begins chattering as we back out of the driveway. As the sun sets on our first day of travel, he's still talking.

"Drink in the scenery, kids. You're seeing America!!!" I look up from *Mad* magazine. Rows of corn. Same scenery as an hour ago. Unmoved, I return to Spy vs. Spy.

We pull into a campground outside of Lincoln, Nebraska. Volkswagen vans with flowers and peace signs painted on their sides are circled like wagons. A sweet-smelling haze hangs over the grounds, and the air is filled with guitar music and Frisbees. As we unload the car, I wish we didn't have the Nixon/Agnew bumper sticker. I feel hopelessly square.

A hippy couple approaches our car. The guy looks like Jesus and the woman has flowers in her hair and hair under her arms.

"Hey man," the guy says, in slow motion, "Can you help us out? We need some pots and pans to cook our fewd."

I fear my dad will lecture them on the dangers of Communism and free love. But to my relief, he engages in friendly small talk like he's in a Mayberry barbershop. With a sleepy, peace-loving smile, the woman thanks my dad and bends down to pick up a pot. To my amazement, a pendulous breast swings out of her dress. Wow. The first live breast I've ever seen. I clear my throat and pretend I didn't see anything. The couple promises to return the cookware in an hour. They wish us peace and disappear. Forever.

After shopping for replacement pots and pans, we begin our climb into the Rockies. Along the way I have a bag of licorice, three strips of beef jerky, and two bottles of Orange Crush. I realize this was a mistake. The winding mountain passes and my dad's ceaseless commentary are too much. My stomach reverses engines. I call for an emergency stop, and bail out of the car. Behind a rock somewhere near the Continental Divide, I cough and wrench and finally feel better. With hands on my knees I look out over the snow-capped scenery while the mountain air cools my sweating face.

We camp outside Aspen in a place so dark I can't see my hand in front of my face. We fall asleep to the sound of rain on the canvas tent. In the morning, I wake up to find that Jean, dad, and the car have vanished. The rain begins again. There's no food, no people in sight. I am left to wonder: Have I been abandoned? Were they abducted? I know my dad is absent-minded. But could he forget me and the tent?

For nearly two hours I contemplate what it will be like to be raised by wolves. Then I hear tires on gravel. My dad apologizes. They went to Mass and it took them a while to find a church. He tells me he did me a favor by letting me sleep. I thank him heartily.

It's the middle of July and the Grand Canyon is an oven. We hike to the bottom. On the way up, my dad staggers like a heavyweight who's getting up after a second knockdown. For the first time in 1,500 miles, he's not talking.

That night, we camp out in Flagstaff. While my dad sips a Cabin Still before dinner, Jean and I play catch. She may not be great conversational company in the car, but she's a terrific baseball companion. Her fastball heats up my glove and causes my fingers to throb. She's the best girl athlete I've ever seen. It's too bad there isn't a team she can play on. Perhaps someday.

In New Mexico we drive for three hours across the desolate plains to get to Four Corners, the place where you can stand in four states at the same time. In the middle of nowhere, I stand on the dusty plaque. As the tumbleweeds blow past, I look around at the nothingness. "Gee, Dad, this sure was worth the drive."

In Oklahoma, we see the guy from the Wheaties boxes, Bob Richards, riding his bike on the highway behind a big General Mills van. He's pedaling across the country, showing the world what Wheaties can do for you. Thinking there's a Minneapolis connection, my dad pulls alongside the smiling athlete and yells out the window, "Bob White, Minneapolis," and gives a wave. Mortified, I slink to the backseat floor.

In Abilene, Kansas, we visit Eisenhower's boyhood home. At the front door, in front of thirty tourists waiting to go through the house, my dad knocks on the door pretending to be an encyclopedia salesman.

On day eleven, I'm suffering from terminal car sickness. I've had enough bonding with my old man and sister to last me until I'm 40. When the skyline of Minneapolis appears in the distance, I'm so happy I could cry.

On the radio they talk about the space mission headed for the moon. What a time to be alive. Man about to walk on the moon. Peace and love and women burning their bras. What could be next?

As we turn down our street, I sense the world will never be the same after this summer. Perhaps by the end of the century, we'll all be flying to the moon, and we can stand there the way I did at the Four Corners. Just go for the sake of going. Yes, the world will be quite a place in the 1990s. I wonder where I'll be.

It's About Time

L int wiggles in the corner of the screen, then suddenly disappears. The projector hums as the image comes into focus. I'm collecting photos for my parents' 50th wedding anniversary and I've found a treasure buried beneath boxes and sleeping bags in a basement closet. Trays and trays of unorganized slides. Pictures I've never seen.

The image is upside down, then backwards before I get it right. It's a cocktail party from the old house. Must be the late '50s. The whole gang is there: my parents and their friends. The women glamorous in their pearls and heels. Like movie stars, they hold lipsticked cigarettes and sit in dresses that fan out. The men in dark suits and thin ties, smiling at the apex of life. Careers on track, they exude the cocky glow of youth.

Everyone holding a highball, caught by the camera, forever in mid-laughter. I can hear them roar:

"Tiger, what are you drinking?"

"Robert, give me a bourbon."

From left to right, I do a head count. He's gone. I remember his funeral too. Among the living I count four widows, three hip replacements, and a pacemaker. Time is a war that takes its toll on both the living and the dead. What gets me most, though, is that every one of those beaming faces on the screen is younger than I am now.

Funny things keep happening to me these days. Like the other night: I walk into my girlfriend's house and people jump out from behind furniture and yell, "Happy Birthday, you old fart!!! How's it feel to be forty?!!"

This is all just a joke, right? I can't be forty. In my heart and mind, I'm still a sophomore, maybe a junior on a mature day.

They give me birthday cards with jokes about limp body parts, extinct urges and failing functions.

And the birthday cake, crowded with candles, gives off heat in waves. By the time I blow out the last candle with a gasp, there's more smoke than a doused camp fire. There are jokes about setting off the smoke alarm. Oh, forty is funny, you bet. Sure, I'll laugh along with the others. But seriously, there must be a typo on the birth certificate.

These days I bump into middle-aged people, impostors who claim we went to grade school together. Like this bald guy droning on about his insurance business. He claims he's Tim Harris, that funny, freckle-faced kid who once threw up in his desk in second grade. But this can't be. This guy's got three kids and hair growing out his ears. It cannot be the same person.

The children of friends also play tricks on me. My friend Jerry's son, for instance. I remember the kid sucking a nook and blowing bubbles out his nose. It seems like a few weeks go by and now he's a lanky young man with a cracking voice. His parents order him to stop on the way out the door and say hello to me. With eyes to the ground he extends an unenthusiastic handshake. For him, this is just another tedious, mandatory encounter with a clueless adult. No, he doesn't remember me, and frankly he doesn't care if I remember him when he was weee high. While I blather on, he edges toward the door.

I search for solace in pop culture, seeking signs that 40 really isn't old. With hope I look to Mick Jagger and the Rolling Stones. They're still on tour! But then I see them interviewed on TV. They look like aged reptiles, the lines on their faces deep as canyons carved in rock. From mescaline to Metamucil—Mick's bad boy strut now looks like a hurried walk to a restroom.

I watch the Olympics and look for contemporaries among the competitors. I am depressed. I find no one is close, not even the ancient Carl Lewis. I have unopened mail that's been around longer than some of the women gymnasts.

Then, on the next to last day of competition, I see an Olympic athlete my age!! But he doesn't run or jump or swim. He's a gray-haired gentleman dressed like he's going to lunch at the Minneapolis Club. He wears a coat and tie and rides a horse. Thank God for the equestrian event. I still have a chance for gold.

Moved by the Olympics, I visit the local track. I want to see if I can run the 400 meters in anything close to a minute. It looks so easy on TV. I begin with a sprint. I feel great—the first 25 yards. At 100 meters my arms are flailing, my breathing comes in wheezes and grunts. Halfway round the track I am out of fuel. I begin decelerating to a jog. By the time I trot to the finish line, Michael Johnson would have taken his medal, showered, and left the stadium.

The big FOUR-Oh. If life is a football game, this is halftime. No, check that. From an actuarial standpoint, the band has left the field, and I'm about six minutes into the third quarter. No, that's not right either. The truth is, if life is a football game, it's sudden death overtime, all the time. The game could end at any moment.

So I've got nothing to lose. I might as well take a good, outrageous risk every day. But I can't just revert to adolescent behavior to celebrate my mid-life crisis. I've been doing that for years. It's time for something really outrageous and different. I won't join a hair club or chase co-eds. No, lately I've been lusting over mini-vans. And tonight I carry a ring in my pocket as I pick up my girlfriend for dinner. She thinks I've been acting odd lately. Well, she hasn't seen anything yet.

The Engagement

The choking, stammering question stumbles and falls from my lips. It lies on the table between us like spilled milk. She looks at me, speechless, an expression of disbelief and horror on her face. I reach for the box in my pocket to prove I wasn't joking. I pull out a handful of lint and a nickel. Wrong pocket.

I shift cheeks. Leaning back, I straighten my leg beneath the table and dig like I'm looking for car keys. Ah, there it is. I extract the gold-wrapped box, turning my pocket inside out, leaving it hanging like a dog ear. I place the tiny box on the table and push it toward her. She stares at it, as if it's a bomb that might go off.

"Go ahead. Open it."

Slowly, she reaches for the box, and, regaining

her sarcastic composure, pushes it aside.

"Did the Twins win today?"

But even she can't joke her way out of the momentousness of the occasion. With hands shaking like a junkie, she fumbles with the bow, her breathing getting tighter as she unwraps the box. She maintains control of her emotions, knowing that, coming from me, a snake could spring from the box.

She pauses a moment before opening the lid. Her eyes closed, she takes a deep breath, then looks inside. Immediate Niagara Falls. The faucet is on. Tears flow. She covers her mouth. Is she going to vomit? Is she in pain?

For once, she can't speak. Her arms flail like she's giving clues in charades. I consider whacking her on the back to jump-start her larynx. Finally, gasping, sniffling, wiping, she regains her ability to speak. She looks at me.

"Let me get back to you in a week."

So now we're engaged. Bridal magazines, thick as phone books, appear. Wedding plans proceed like a military buildup. We begin Reagan-style deficit spending.

Though the asking was my doing, from here on, it's her show. I'm Ed McMahon to her Johnny Carson. Life has prepared her perfectly for the role. But I am totally lost. I'm told where to go, when to be there, and how to dress.

Instinctively she knows how to exhibit the ring. She extends her arm into a circle of curious females, stretching her fingers until they arch. The group gathers around the ring like it's a newborn. They ooohhh and aaahhh and inspect it up close. They share ring stories. On the couch I flip to ESPN. From across the room I'm congratulated for picking such a nice ring. I hit the mute button. "Huh?" but it doesn't matter. Their attention is back on ring things.

Today we're in a place I never knew existed: the china department in Dayton's. We're registering for wedding gifts. I walk sideways through rows and rows of useless, fragile, expensive stuff, trying not to break things. Linda wants my opinion on the herringbone. I don't know a herringbone from a thighbone. I say, "Whatever is fine with me."

I look longingly at the bank of televisions next door at the electronics department. A wall full of sets, each tuned to sports. Perhaps I could wait there while Linda chooses patterns. I suggest this option. I'm voted down like a third-party candidate. It's important to her that I have an opinion on these matters. But I have no opinion. I have no knowledge. I would be better suited to captain a submarine than comment on china.

We move on to bedding. She asks my views on thread count. Me? Thread count? I rotate my tires more often than I wash my sheets. I've got a towel I've used since college. Linen issues are not high on my list of concerns. I say whatever she likes, I like. Can we go now? She ignores me.

I chase her through flatware. I try hard to care. I study spoons. I ding the crystal. I use shopping adjectives I've never used before: "Oh, that is lovely. So understated. Quite elegant." I even let the word "cute" slip from my lips.

I rack up big points for patience and enthusiasm. But I can't keep it up. There is no way I can match her shopping endurance. In housewares I feel like I can't take it any longer. As she ponders garlic presses for fifteen minutes I'm feeling cranky, like a child who hasn't had a nap. She consoles me, assures me we won't have to shop tomorrow. That's because tomorrow evening we have a couples shower!

A video camera sits on a tripod, aimed at us as we open presents. We're knee-deep in wrapping and I'm concerned because I can't find my beer. The next gift is opened. Linda triumphantly raises it over her head like it's the Stanley Cup. I ask what it is. It appears to me to be a crystal thing.

Linda shouts a thank you across the room to the hard-of-hearing Aunt Mary. I locate my beer. Happily, I wave my beer at Aunt Mary, thanking her for that beautiful crystal thing.

The next day is a perfect day for golf. But there will be no golf for me. No sir. This evening we must attend the first of our mandatory marriage encounter sessions. I moan and complain as we walk across the church parking lot. We bid good-bye to the flawless summer evening, and descend into the stale, flat light of the fluorescently lit church basement. A sign at the door says, "Welcome engaged couples!"

We join thirty other couples seated on folding chairs in a large circle. Next to us, a nervous bride-to-be snuggles against her fiancé as if he's a large pillow. He stares straight ahead like a man condemned to die.

The retreat leader enters. I am gripped with fear that he'll make us join hands and sing "Kumbaya." Instead, he instructs us to go off with our partner and discuss relationship issues such as how we communicate, how we deal with anger, money and football on TV. We go off to a quiet corner. We take each other's hands, look into one another's eyes, and make fun of the other members of our class.

The planning is over. I stand at the back of the church in my rented shoes. Shiny, black, plastic shoes. The most important day of my life, and I'm wearing the ugliest shoes I've ever seen. I guess it's just tradition. But all this doesn't matter to me anymore. The music begins. Butterflies jump in my stomach, but I'm not afraid. I'm feeling very lucky today.

Nye Night

T he neighbors suspect I've got bodies in the trunk. But it's just 400 pounds of soggy sand to help me on the ice. Without it, my car has the traction of an excited dog on a hardwood floor.

It's snowing again. I turn in to the alley. This could be a mistake. With my rear end dragging in the snow, if I slow down to less than 30 I'm stuck. There's no turning back. Up ahead, my driveway has an ice bump at the entry the size of a pitcher's mound. Maybe I can jump it if I get up enough speed. I press the garage door opener and hit the accelerator. I feel like Evel Knievel at Caesar's Palace.

The car bottoms out. Crrrr. My muffler is punished by the ice mound. I fishtail into the driveway and slide into the garage. Safe at home.

I walk in the door. My wife is putting away the crackers she had for dinner. This reminds me: We were supposed to go out to dinner tonight. In fact, about an hour and a half ago. I guess I sort of forgot. That's because my brain seems to clear out its memory banks every twenty minutes or so. I could tell you who was American League MVP in 1965, but dinner plans made yesterday just don't seem to leave an impression.

I stammer in defense. I blame my watch, the weather, the dog. I apologize, explain, and finally improvise. Okay, dinner's out. It's too late for a movie and too snowy to drive. But I have an idea. We live in Northeast Minneapolis. What is Nordeast famous for? Bars. Let's call a cab and go out for a drink!

Twenty minutes later, the cab pulls up. The cabby looks like Tommy Lasorda before Slim Fast. His chubby arm clung over the seat, he leans back, two fingers on the wheel beneath his belly. From the back seat I lean forward like a school kid on a field trip. I ask all the questions that people who don't take cabs often ask: How's business? Ever pick up any weirdos? You ever afraid? Gosh, the cabby even lets me feel the lead-pipe flashlight he keeps under his seat for protection. The radio squawks. He talks back as we swing in front of the bar.

The front door to Nye's bursts open. Music

from the piano bar spills onto the street. Arm in arm, a love-drunk couple meanders their way out into the night, their voices as loud as the man's plaid slacks.

Inside, the air is dense with noise and smoke. My contacts shrivel in protest as we pinball our way through the broad-shouldered crowd. We wedge in at the corner of the bar. Above us, a silent television is tuned to a fight nobody is watching.

Behind the piano sits Lou, the musical legend of Northeast Minneapolis. She hits a high note. She looks like she's gargling. Her mouth is a giant square as she forms vowels. With lips pulled back, she reveals a set of gums Mr. Ed would envy. In her off-key, Ethel Merman voice, she belts it out.

Those were the days my friend,

we thought they'd never end.

Gathered at the piano, the regulars lean hunch-shouldered over drinks with sad smiles on their faces. The song ends and one of them sets down his cigarette and grabs the microphone. His toupee looks like it fell on his head from a second story window. There's a great huffy burst of wind as he holds the microphone beneath his nose and gathers himself for his performance.

He croons low and off-key.

Yesterday. All my troubles seemed so far away.

At a table in the center of the bar is an island of youth. Four women in their twenties, students from the University perhaps, settle into their seats, arranging their purses and shaking free of overcoats. They look around, wide-eyed as does, taking in the authentic tackiness that has evolved into chic. Huddled together, they whisper and giggle and point in awe at the '70s paneling, the sparkling gold vinyl booths and the blue-collar Liberace with the microphone.

To the shark across the bar their presence is blood upon the water. His shirt collar spread open, gold chains on his wrist, he is a smooth operator. Rico Suavé. He picks up his drink and glides through the bar as if he's balancing a tray on his head. He circles the table, eyeing his prey, composing his line.

He swoops in. The women stiffen as if there's a bee in their presence. He leans into their space, lays his charm on the table and waits for their swooning presence. The table greets him like the flu. Unfazed, he stands back up, adjusting a tie that isn't there, and floats on to the next opportunity.

After two Brain Melts, er, Grain Belts, I get curious about Manhattans because the guy next to me is drinking one. I convince my wife, who is still working on her first glass of wine, that a Manhattan would be really good for me.

The first one disappears before I finish making the point I was making about the economy. The second one carries me through the issues of crime, welfare reform and the techniques of wallpaper removal. I don't recall ordering the third but there it is and what the heck. I don't have to drive. Here's to Friday nights in Northeast Minneapolis!

Now I get up to go to the bathroom. I must have had a slight stroke at the bar because I can't feel my face. As I weave through the crowd, it feels like the good ship Nye's is in rough seas. When I finally locate the men's room, I try pushing the wall instead of the bathroom door.

When I return to the bar, my wife has gathered up our coats. As we make our way towards the door, a woman takes up the microphone. She looks too timid to speak, much less sing. She could be a librarian. Maybe she still lives at home with her parents and this is the highlight of her life. But when she starts to sing, the place becomes quiet for a moment.

We step outside into the snowy evening and wait. From inside, above the laughter and the cursing, we still can hear that one sweet voice.

An Excellent Adventure

S ince my buddy Tom has a car, and Rich and Doug and I all have our driver's licenses now that we're sixteen, it seems the smart thing to do this spring break is to drive to Florida. The rest of the guys have already convinced their parents to let them go. But when they show up at my house on Friday after school, I haven't yet brought up the subject with my mom and dad.

Tom's '62 Chevy Impala, loaded with suitcases and camping gear, painfully scrapes the pavement as he turns in to our driveway; and when he applies the brakes, the car rocks like it has old bedsprings for shocks. Tom turns off the engine but the motor continues to fight for life, pinging and coughing before finally expiring with a wheeze.

Rich kicks open the passenger door. The squeaky door makes a series of vowel sounds as it swings open. With his Twins cap on backwards, Rich jumps out of the car and bellows in a voice loud enough for the entire neighborhood to hear, "C'mon, White, let's go. Let's get the f@#*#@# outta here and party!!!"

My mother, clutching a sweater, steps out to the driveway to see what's going on. From the back seat, Doug Schwab rolls down the window and gives her an Eddie Haskell greeting, "Hello, Mrs. White, how are you this evening?"

Circling the vehicle like a customs officer, my mother observes the tent and sleeping bags tied to the top of the car. She begins her interrogation, "So what do you boys think you're up to?"

There is an uncomfortable moment of silence, followed by some shuffling and stammering, and finally I blurt out our travel plans. But before I can say "Daytona Beach," the plan is vetoed.

"Absolutely not, no way."

"But mom…"

"End of discussion. Good-bye, boys." She heads back into the house to finish fixing dinner. Just then, the trip's last hope arrives. My dad pulls into the driveway, waving at us like a man running for office. Mr. Easy has arrived.

I plead my case as I help him unload the samples from his car. Sixteen is plenty old, I argue, and Frey's already had his license for almost a year. Then I accidentally stumble into the magic of selling through metaphor, thanks to some required reading in my American Lit class.

"It's like…Huck Finn going down the river," I blurt out. "Think of this as my trip down the river. It's an experience." The apple-pie image captures my dad's imagination. The light goes on in his eyes and I know he's sold. He lobbies my mother. She never actually agrees to let me go, but being so badly outnumbered she really has no choice.

We tie more luggage onto the top of the car and the transmission drops with a "lunk" into reverse. My parents stand side by side, waving from the driveway. My dad looks as though he's waving to his son on the football field, but my mother waves sadly, like she's sending a son off to war.

In Wisconsin, Frey gets a speeding ticket. In Illinois, we get lost on a country road and Frey attempts a U-turn that leaves us stuck in a ditch. It's past midnight when Schwab and I bang on the door of a nearby farmhouse. The kindly old farmer wipes the sleep from his eyes and pulls us out of the ditch with his tractor.

Finally we reach Daytona Beach. We set up our tent on a beachfront campground and go out for our fifth consecutive meal at McDonald's.

When we return, our tent and sleeping bags are gone. After blaming each other, then finally deciding it must be Frey's fault, we go in search of the cheapest motel we can find. After Schwab and Garretty check in, promising the clerk it's just the two of them, Frey and I crawl in the window of the closet-sized room and the four of us settle in for our first night in Florida.

The next day somebody tells us Fort Lauderdale is the place to be. So we drive there and pull into the first parking space we can find near the beach. The four of us, squinty eyed and pasty, sprint and hop over waves, into the foaming surf of the Atlantic. We spend the day throwing the Frisbee in the water. By afternoon, Garretty's fish-belly skin has turned most of the hues of the rainbow. The next day, shivering with sunburn, Garretty visits the outpatient unit of the local hospital.

All week, the four of us fail miserably in our attempts to meet girls. Most are college age and brush us off like pesky younger brothers. We also fail in our attempts to sneak into bars, until one night, to our surprise, we are welcomed into a bar called the Driftwood. When the bartender lays four napkins in front of us, my brain locks and I can't remember the name of a single drink. Thankfully, Garretty has the presence of mind to order a seven-and-seven. I follow suit, having no idea what I'm ordering.

As Stevie Wonder's "You Are the Sunshine of My Life" plays, my first real drink in public arrives. What a great place! I say to myself. But, gee, how odd. There's not a single girl here. What are the chances of that? An overly tanned man in white shorts and shoes takes the seat next to me and nearly purrs, "Hello," with a prolonged emphasis on the second syllable. I elbow the ribs of the oblivious Frey next to me and pull my confused friends out of the bar like the place is on fire.

On the street, lit pink and green in neon, we look at each other in amazement. How bizarre this all is. As we make our way down the boulevard, Lou Reed's Take a Walk on the Wild Side can be heard from the open windows of a slowly passing car: "I said hey, babe, take a walk on the wild side."

Toward the end of the thirty-six-hour ride home, I sit slumped in the back seat thinking about what a great trip we had. An experience I wouldn't trade for anything.

Back in Minneapolis the phone rings with the terrible news. My sister's boyfriend calls and tells her he heard on the radio that four guys from Edina High School were in a car accident while driving back from spring break. One of the four died. And one of the four is named Frey. "Wasn't your brother with a guy named Frey?"

My sister cries hysterically. My dad leads the family in the Rosary. My mother frantically calls to get more information. They wait for the phone to ring. It never does. Instead, the back door flies open.

Greasy from a showerless two days of travel, I toss down my sand-filled duffle bag, and call out to the darkened house. My family rushes in, amazingly pleased to see me. What's going on? I wonder. Tom Sawyer comes to mind again: Like him, I feel as though I've walked into my own funeral.

As it turns out, the accident involved a classmate of mine named Jim Frey. He lost a friend in the accident, and the use of his legs for life.

Twenty-four years later I'm walking to the office, my head filled with the usual trivial angst that marks our modern life. "Let's see, I've got to call the travel agent today, and damn, I forgot to stop by the dry cleaners, and oh, boy, I bet I've got e-mail up the ying yang."

At the corner of Sixth and Marquette I run into Jim Frey. A successful lawyer and businessman now, he looks sharp in his suit. Looking up at me from his wheelchair, he somehow looks wise and serene. We chat for a moment. Then the light turns green and we go our separate ways. I walk. He rolls.

As I cross the street, for a moment my petty concerns are put on hold. There, in the middle of Marquette Avenue, I feel a sudden and simple gratitude for my very steps upon the earth.

Party Time

In a half-hour, the guests will arrive. I jump in the shower and grab the razor-thin sliver of what used to be a bar of soap. It melts in my hands before it yields lather. As a soap substitute, I reach for the half gallon container of discount shampoo that has lasted me a year.

The hair-clogged drain is on strike again, and by the time I'm done with the shower I'm ankle-deep in old water. I close the mildew-laden shower curtain to hide from the guests the little Lake Erie in my tub.

Now to prepare the spread. The pretzels go in soup bowls, but I need something bigger for the large, orange ranch-style Dorito chips. Ah-hah. That fruit bowl that currently holds a month's worth of unopened mail is perfect. I toss the mail in the linen closet and fill the bowl with chips.

I jam bottles of beer in the snow out back, and set out the jugs of screw-top wine. For drinkware, I offer my guests a wide variety of choices: glasses and plastic cups from Arby's, A&W, Super America, the Twins, the Vikings and an invitational golf tournament I don't remember playing in. Add to this thirteen law firm coffee mugs and the Styrofoam cups I found in the cupboard above the refrigerator when I moved into this place, and I think we're set.

I insert a homemade Neil Young tape into the stereo and just as the doorbell rings, I lower the lights, and kick the laundry under the bed. It's party time.

That was then. This is now.

Party preparations began three weeks ago. It's as if we're having the Pope over for cocktails. Two days ago, my wife handed me a written list of things to do. Twenty-seven simple tasks, all within my skill level. Most involve lifting or moving something heavy. None requires taste or particular ability.

It's T-minus two hours to party time and I'm moving chairs up from the basement, cursing the door jamb that just scraped my knuckle. Next I carry bags of ice in from the car, then I clean and set up the barbecue. Now I'm on to my final chore.

I push the button on the vacuum cleaner and the dog nearly suffers a nervous breakdown. The cowering canine backpedals in front of me, and manages to move to every spot I'm trying to vacuum. Finally, I'm done. The dog, relieved that I'm no longer chasing him around with this strange appliance, happily follows me downstairs to the bathroom.

I have thirty minutes to shower and shave before I'm barred from the bathroom. Once I vacate the facility, the area will be sanitized and made guest worthy.

I step into the shower and face a rack full of my wife's mysterious skin and hair products. I have no idea what any of these are for. There's a hair detoxifier, a volumizer, a diffusor, a reconstructor and a detangler. Even the conditioner, the one product I'm familiar with, is not just a conditioner, but a "hypothermic bonding conditioner."

Most of the major food groups are represented in our shower. There's a sun-ripened raspberry and almond body scrub with apricot seeds; a honey and pear moisturizing body wash fortified with vitamin E; and a bar of oatmeal and sunflower oil soap.

On the labels, herbal-speak abounds: "Made from organically grown herbs and natural clarifiers." And of course, what's an overpriced, American-made bath product without the French to make it all official? "Reconstituant qui demele tous les types de cheveux." It all sounds like something off an expensive menu.

I ignore all these and reach for my trusty Suave brand shampoo and conditioner in one: nothing fancy on this label, except the banner that proclaims excitedly, "Now with 20% more!!!"

Twenty minutes until the party. I look around the house. I am struck by how perfect the place looks. Every trace of my existence has been carefully hidden from view. Stashed behind the straining closet doors are piles of my athletic gear, clothes for Goodwill, stacks of magazines and un-recycled newspapers. The small mountain of receipts and unsorted mail on my desk has been stuffed in drawers that may never open again.

In place of reality, a perfect cuteness abounds. The spread of hors d'oeuvres looks like a layout for a *Bon Appetit* cover shot. Misty wedding photos are displayed next to a vase of fresh cut flowers. On the white linen tablecloth is crystal stemware I didn't know we owned. And throughout the house, there are more lit candles than a Latin high mass.

I hover over the hors d'oeuvre table and make a selection. An olive tumbles to the floor where the dog scoops up the rebound. I wolf down a little salmon paté thing. Half lands on my foot. Just as the dog is licking my shoe, my wife enters.

To her, at this crucial moment, we represent only spillage, breakage, and other potential disasters. Thus, we are banished from the house until the guests arrive.

Outside the dog raises a leg against the shrubs, his breath lit by the autumn moon. I pick up his tennis ball and toss it into the yard two houses down. The black dog disappears into the night. After a moment, a rustling of leaves and the panting of breath mark his invisible return. He circles me, tail wagging and drops the ball into the cool grass inviting me to throw it again.

He and I, the primitive males in the moonlit yard. I look toward the house. From inside I hear the nervous heels on the hardwood floor as final preparations are made. Then, at last, there is music. The civilized sounds of Frank Sinatra and a warm glowing light emanate out the windows of the house—the house she has made a home. Around the front of the house, I see the first car pulling up. It's safe for us to go inside. I scratch myself and the dog lifts his leg, then together, we head back into the light.

Mass Appeal

The heavy church door slams behind me. So much for sneaking quietly into Mass. After a spirited Saturday night, I've overslept and am very late for the 11 a.m. service.

I haven't showered or shaved and I look like I'm ready to check into the Betty Ford Clinic. I just want to stand, unseen, in the back of the church. But it's too late. The overly efficient ushers, hovering like Secret Service agents in the rear of the church, have spotted me. I lamely decline their invitation to seat me, but they're determined to find me a place whether I like it or not.

A smiling, cologne-soaked usher approaches. With a hand placed gently on my back, he guides me along the back of the church to the center aisle. I feel like a criminal being led into court.

Halfway up the aisle another usher has a seat for me. He waves me forward like a ground crew worker guiding a jet onto the runway. I don't want to sit way up there. I slept on my head funny. From the front I look like Cosmo Kramer and from the back, it looks like half my skull is missing, my hair is so badly matted. But after all the gesturing by the usher, I have no choice. I march up the aisle. Every head in church turns wondering who the Unabomber look-alike is.

I whisper a weak apology to the entire row, which has to slide down one seat to make room for me. I settle into the creaky pew next to a woman who regards me as if I were a contagious fungus. Just as my rear touches the seat, it's time to stand for the gospel. Ah, the up and down, stand, sit, kneel aerobics of church.

I grab a missal and try to figure out what page we're on. It's no use. I have to sneak a peek at the book of the woman beside me. Looking over her shoulder, I feel like I'm cheating on an exam. I finally locate the passage just as the priest concludes, "This is the word of the Lord." Now it's time to sit for the sermon. Father clears his throat into the microphone.

"Brothers and sisters in Christ..."

Within two sentences, my attention drifts away like smoke. Up, up, up to the top of the great marble dome above the altar. I gaze at the distant lights. I wonder how they change those light bulbs way up there? I wonder if I could throw a baseball that high. Who do the Wolves play next? When's my next oil change?

I snap out of it, and try to refocus on the words of the priest.

"And it is this sense of fellowship with the spirit that leads us to…"

In the seat in front of me, a little girl drools on a rattle and stares at me. Why is she transfixed on me? Hasn't she ever seen a man with half a head? I'm made slightly uncomfortable by her gaze. I smile at her and mouth the word "helloooeew." Big mistake. She babbles gleefully in return, her little voice echoing off the great stone walls of the church. She extends to me her saliva-soaked toy as a gift. Thankfully, her mother gathers her up in her arms and glances at me as if somehow I was egging the child on.

The sermon completed, we stand to say the Apostles' Creed. An elderly woman nearby recites the prayer loudly, lagging behind the rest of us by a line or two. Her spirited voice is like an echo, repeating what the rest of us said five seconds earlier.

"Now let us extend to one another the sign of God's peace," says the priest.

It's that slightly awkward, obligatory social moment. The most post-Vatican II part of the

Mass, but one of my personal favorites: the kiss of peace.

I turn around and extend my hand to a teenage kid wearing Nike high tops and a letter jacket. Without eye contact, he reluctantly extends his hand, like a child being forced to shake and make up after a fight. "Peace be with you," I say. "Peace…" he mumbles back.

"Peace be with you. Peace. Peace to you." I shake hands with everyone in the vicinity. I feel like I'm running for Senate. I shake the thick, dry hands of blue-collar workers; the icy, gnarled hands of the elderly; the soft, moist palms of the young. I wave and nod, I stop just short of kissing babies. Throughout the church, there are smiles. But the buzz gradually simmers down. The party is over. The hard, unforgiving old wooden kneelers groan as the congregation settles to its knees.

The little old Apostles' Creed lady clutches a rosary, her lips moving in silent prayer. She knows why she is here. Her faith is simple and sure. But what am I doing here? Didn't college teach me that religion is merely the opiate of the masses?

A little boy suddenly steps out into the aisle, and gleefully races toward the back of the church. His mother in high heels runs on tiptoes to capture the little escapee. She scoops him up, and the boy cries and squirms like he's trying to slither out of a straitjacket.

I can relate to the kid. I used to hate being forced to sit still in church. I remember doing anything I could to break up the torture of mass: whistling during moments of silence; stepping into the aisle and bowing at the women returning from communion; mimicking the priest during all-school masses; anything to get a laugh.

Here I am, thirty-some years later, and I'm still restless in the pew. I'd rather be home, drinking coffee, reading the Sunday paper, watching the political talk shows and football on Fox. So why am I here? Is it good old-fashioned Catholic guilt and a sense of obligation? Or is it a desire to know God, to reflect on life, atone for sins, and develop spiritually? Or am I just covering myself in case admission to heaven is really based in part on church attendance?

I'm not sure. It might be all those reasons. I glance at my watch. I'm going to miss the kickoff of the Packers game. Maybe I should sneak out early after communion. But a voice inside me tells me to stay put, that it's somehow a good thing to be here. For just this one hour, the voice says, be quiet, and just be still.

Skyway to Heaven

It's morning rush hour in the skyway. The arteries of the city are clogged with humanity. Women in Nikes and nylons rush to the office. Caribou-mug-bearing zombies walk trance-like in search of their first cup. And in everyone's way, the maintenance guy with the carpet sweeper pursuing that one piece of popcorn.

Caffeinated, wired, and ready to go, I've got my list of things to do, my priorities set, my people to call. I have a nine o'clock, a ten o'clock, a lunch and a Day-Timer bleeding with notes and lists. I'm at that point in life where crossing items off my to-do list is a huge thrill.

Bobbing in and out of traffic, I'm doing the skyway weave. Dangerously passing on the left, avoiding the oncoming skyway traffic.

Back in my lane, I get caught in a slow-moving pack. Jockeying for position, I wait for an opening, then pass on the outside, taking an elbow on the way. It's like the Roller Derby out here. Free of the pack now, I continue on my way, full speed ahead.

Suddenly, there is a slowdown in the skyway. I slam on the brakes, and go up on tiptoes, nearly trampling the woman in front of me. What the—? Up ahead, I see the problem. An old man shuffles along, leaning heavily on his cane. Like a slow-moving tractor on a highway, he is causing a major pileup.

The old man now applies his brittle body hopelessly against a set of heavy skyway doors. Several of us help him battle the doors open against the skyway breeze. With a whoosh, we burst through the doors like agents on a drug raid. With a trailing foot and a perfunctory smile, I hold the door open for the old man, then hurry on my way.

It's not until I'm in the next skyway that his face registers. It's in those old photos of my parents' parties—those great bashes of the '50s and '60s. I can still hear the booming laughter, the off-key singing, the tinkling of ice cubes in highball glasses. I see my parents and their friends, their faces beaming with youth and promise. The men with their arms around each other, grinning and gesturing through the blue smoke, caught mid-sentence, or mid-laughter, frozen forever in the moment by the surprise flash. His was one of those faces.

Now the ranks of friends are depleted, like soldiers under siege. Just a handful of the crowd survives. A generation disappearing. Tom Brokaw calls them "the Greatest Generation," that World War II, hard-living, anything-is-possible-so-let's-go-to-the-moon generation. Such a far cry from the cautious, low-fat, mandatory-helmet-wearing generation we've become.

I stop and look for the old man through the crowd. Unnoticed by the passers-by, he turns a corner and totters off. I watch until he disappears, as if I'm catching the last glimpse of a setting sun. I turn and continue on my way.

But the bounce is gone from my step. Should I backtrack and say hello? I try to convince myself it's not worth it. I have e-mail and voicemail and U.S. mail to go through. Besides, would he even know who I am? I haven't seen him in years. To him I'm probably just one of the kids in pajamas saying good night to the adults.

Not only that, but he probably never really knew my name. Back then, all the families had six or seven kids. The adults never could get our names right. They'd call us by the names of our siblings until they eventually stumbled upon ours—"Hello…Jimmy…Bobby…er…Billy…"

But a nagging guilt works on me. I turn around and go after him. I call out his name. He turns slowly in my direction—the stiff shoulder, full-body turn of the elderly. His eyes wide in bewilderment. But his expression of concern slowly melts into a smile of recognition. He says only one brother's name before he gets mine right.

"How're your folks?" he asks. "Boy, we used to have fun. And your dad, what a nut," he says, shaking his head at the memories. "How's he doing? You know, I've got the same ticker problem he has, only his is worse."

Shifting on his cane, he continues, "Great guy, your old man," he says. "Yeah, probably the greatest guy I've ever known," he says, looking at me to be sure I know he's not pulling my leg. "Say hello to your folks for me."

On the way to the office, I think of my parents. How they made it over to our house for a party the other night. A major undertaking for them, navigating the snowy streets.

My dad, due to medications and a lack of steadiness on his feet, moves in perpetual slow motion. Half the time he can't make it to the worsh room, as he calls it. Tonight is no different. He gets out of the car, and stands in the street, answering nature's call. Throughout the slow drain, he keeps the chatter going.

"Wowee, kid!" he sighs his relief into cold, night air. With age comes freedom. He couldn't care less what anyone sees or hears.

And forever the comedian. "Don't look, kid," he says to me. "You'll only get jealous." As he zips up, he continues the patter. "Hey, did I tell you? The doctor only gave me six months to live. But I didn't pay his bill, so he gave me another six months!"

My mother, seemingly forever young, shakes her head and waits for him on the curb. I grab him by the elbow, and point out a patch of ice to watch. But he keeps on talking as I help him up on the walk. "That reminds me," he says to my mother, "Whatever you do, Junie, don't pay that bill…ever!!!"

"The greatest guy I've ever known." The words still resonate in my head as I sit down at my desk. In some skyway of the future, no one will ever remember me for the meetings I attended, or how much correspondence I churned out. But if some friend were to say these words about me to a child of mine, what a big, sparkling success this brief time will have been.

Like a Rolling Stone

Ohne Saturday, shortly after we moved into the neighborhood, my wife was in the yard potting some plants when suddenly she looked up from her work to see a man standing on the front sidewalk, staring at her. He was shabbily dressed and mumbling to himself and had a strange smile on his face. When he began to move up the sidewalk toward her, she gathered up her things and ran inside, locking the door behind her.

As I listen to her story, I'm thinking maybe she's making a big deal out of nothing. Sometimes she overreacts to things. Like if a bee is nearby, her central nervous system kicks into 9-1-1 mode. She'll scream and run around in circles, fanning her head like her hair is on fire.

But then a couple of nights later, around 11,

I'm in the yard surveying the stars while the dog does his business. Suddenly I hear a noise behind me. Footsteps in the darkness. I turn and see a man walking up the street. He's mumbling to himself. Something about the anti-Christ. And while he is talking, he stares at me, grinning maniacally. I rush inside to tell my wife.

"That's him!" my wife says in response to my description.

A couple of days later, I'm up before dawn putting the recycling on the curb for pickup. A London fog has settled gloomily and eerily on the street. A bag of bottles rips open. The aftermath of Saturday night's party rolls onto the street. As I chase a gin bottle, I look up to see the man at the end of our street, standing under a streetlight watching me.

By the time I finish my pickup and look again, he has disappeared into the fog like the ghost of Hamlet's father.

A week later, we're walking home from a movie. A storm is moving in. A block from home, the first, fat drops of rain splat the sidewalk like ripe fruit falling from the heavens. The air is thick and redolent with the smell of the coming rain.

We sprint up the road and turn the corner on our street and suddenly find ourselves face to face with the man. Oblivious to the impending storm, he smiles at us, as if mocking our hurry to get out of the harmless rain. Is he not affected by rain, we wonder?

He's become Boo Radley to us. And we're Scout and Jem concocting all sorts of theories about this strange and ubiquitous presence in our neighborhood.

But the true story of this man is better than anything we could make up.

For more than forty years this man, known around town as Mr. Jimmy, has been walking the streets of Excelsior. A savant, he recites pages of history text as he goes about his harmless way.

On June 12, 1964, he wandered into Bacon Drug on the corner of Second and Water and, as legend has it, stepped into rock 'n' roll history.

On that day, a British band called the Rolling Stones was in town to play up the street at Danceland. A mere 283 people attended the concert.

Some say the band was booed off the stage. Others claim they were threatened in the parking lot afterward by gang members. At any rate, it was by all accounts an inauspicious start to the band's first U.S. tour of nine cities.

Almost everyone I know from that generation claims to have had tickets to this nearly mythical event, but for some reason decided not to go at the last minute. My brother is one of these people. It remains one of his great regrets in life.

In any event, at some point during their

time in Excelsior, Mick Jagger stopped by Bacon Drug and encountered a dejected soul at the soda fountain, who introduced himself as Mr. Jimmy.

Jagger commented that he looked pretty down. Mr. Jimmy explained that he had ordered a cherry soda but didn't get what he wanted and they wouldn't take it back. Turning to Jagger he said, "You can't always get what you want."

Jagger then wrote the song that mentions the same verse, a drug store, a cherry soda, a Mr. Jimmy who looked pretty ill, and of course, the refrain and title, "You can't always get…"

For forty years, the town has looked after Jimmy. Every Christmas season, on the first Saturday of December, someone sees to it that Jimmy gets all cleaned up and shaven and dons a tuxedo. Before the lights on Water Street are lit, he sings *White Christmas*.

This morning, I drive down the main street of Excelsior on my way to work, lost in consternation over the upcoming day. As I pull up to the stop sign, I look over and see Jimmy. He's sitting on a bench, basking in the morning sun like a cat. He looks at me and smiles. Or is he laughing?

The light turns green and I'm on my way. While the rest of us hurry by, endlessly trying to get what we want, Jim shuffles along, day and night, going nowhere in particular.

The Saab Whisperer

A fter two very expensive weeks in the shop, our Saab still runs like a patient on a respirator. The mechanics tell us it's hopeless, that the car will never run right. Though they can't identify the exact problem, they all advise us to junk the car even though it's barely middle-aged in Saab years.

Desperate, I find myself in a part of town famous for drive-by shootings and crack deals. I'm searching for a tiny one-man repair shop recommended by a lawyer who swears by this mechanic. "He eats and drinks Saabs," the lawyer says. "And even if he can't fix your car, it's worth the trip to meet this guy."

Despite the fact there's no sign out front, the

place is easy to spot. Saabs fill every inch of the tiny parking lot, and spill out onto the street. The congregation of luxury automobiles is a strange sight in this neighborhood of dragging tailpipes.

There's no front entry to speak of, just a heavy steel door that requires a shoulder to push open.

I walk inside, and make my way around a clutter of car parts and partially dismantled Saabs. I hear voices in the back.

In the back, I find a yuppie standing beside his car, a suit coat slung over his shoulder. A pair of legs protrudes out the driver's side door. The mechanic belonging to the legs finally slithers out from beneath the dash, holding the car radio in his hands.

The mechanic sits up and shakes shoulder-length hair out of his face. He looks a little like Jim Morrison of The Doors. He wears a hands-free phone set on his head and surgical gloves on his hands.

"Who installed this?" he demands of the customer, holding up the radio.

The man, stammering like a kid called into the principal's office, says meekly, "BBB-Best Buy. Bbbut they installed it for free."

An expression of pain and disgust crosses the mechanic's face. I'm waiting for him to throw the radio against the wall.

"Don't ever, EVER, let those assholes at Best Buy touch a stereo. I don't care about the free installation. I will pay you, man, PAY YOU!!—OUT OF MY OWN POCKET!!!—not to let those assholes touch your car!!!"

He then says he'll fix the stereo and dismisses the customer. Mortified but grateful, the man sheepishly slinks out of the shop.

Now it's my turn.

"Hi, my name is Bill," I say as politely as I know how. "I called earlier..." But the mechanic ignores me, still looking upset at the last customer. He walks past me as if I were invisible, and continues out the shop door.

Left standing among the car parts, I wait for a moment, then realize he's not coming back. I go outside and find him walking around my car. He mumbles something.

"Excuse me?" I say, almost apologetically.

"Pop the hood," he orders.

I get in the car and nervously search for the hood release, thinking to myself, "Nice to meet you too, buddy."

The mechanic lifts the hood and looks at the engine. His face darkens with disappointment and impatience, as if he's been told his flight is canceled.

"Who's the asshole who put this cheap piece-of-crap radiator in?"

I feel like he's blaming me, personally, for this atrocity. Now I'm the one stammering. "I, I, just had it replaced last summer," I say, fumbling through the maintenance file I brought along, trying to find the culprit.

He continues his recitation of wrongs, sounding more like a prosecutor than a mechanic. "The battery's the wrong size for a Saab, and so are the belts. The distributor is a joke. Your left front fender has been repaired and whoever did it is a fu--ing butcher and should NEVER be allowed to touch a Saab."

For a moment he is silent, looking wounded by the desecration of the sacred Saab.

After a moment, he gathers himself. "Start it up."

He looks down upon the wheezing engine in almost a meditative state. Then, gathering his hippy hair behind his head to keep it clear of the fan belt and other moving parts, he places his ear next to the engine, like a doctor listening to a patient's heart.

After a minute of this, he stands up and delivers his diagnosis in a Joe Friday rapid-fire monotone.

"I hear a low-level vibration that concerns me. It could be a bearing. If it's a bearing you're fu--ed and you have a very expensive—but nice looking—pile of scrap metal on your hands. But that's remote. In fifteen years I've only seen one bearing go on a Saab. These engines are bullet-proof and if treated properly should run forever. My hunch is the vibration is a symptom, not a cause. If I need to, I'll turn your engine upside down to find the problem. And when I do, I'll fix it."

I leave his shop, skeptical but hopeful.

That afternoon he calls. His message is deadpan, to the point and completely devoid of pleasantries.

"Come get your car. It's a Saab again," he says simply.

My wife and I drive to the shop. To our amazement, the car runs perfectly. (And has for the past several months. In fact, it runs better than it did the day we bought it.) I'm ready to fall to the ground in gratitude. "What was the problem?" I ask.

"I made one simple adjustment," he says. "The engine timing could not have been farther off if you tried. This was Car Repair 101."

He looks off in the distance, shaking his head in amused exasperation. "Fu--ing amazing what passes for service these days."

It's as if he's condemning not just the mechanics who worked on our car, but an entire culture of incompetence and poor service.

I reach for my wallet, so grateful I'm ready to

pay anything. "What do I owe you?"

"No charge," he says, walking away. I follow him, protesting. But he continues into the shop, talking to himself. Then I realize he's on his hands-free phone talking to his next customer.

"What year is it?" he says, snapping on his surgical gloves. "Bring it in and I'll look at it. But don't let those guys touch it. They're idiots."

The heavy steel door shuts behind him, leaving my wife and me standing in front of the faceless shop, this Lourdes for Saabs. The service without a smile leaves us speechless. We look at each other, utterly amazed by the simple fact that this guy knows his stuff, and our car is fixed.

Raking

The Saturday paper lands with a thump and a skid upon the front sidewalk. My stomach tightens a little as I ponder what might be news today.

I let the dog out and sit on the front steps scanning the apocalyptic headlines, then turn to the sports and variety sections for solace.

The dog rolls happily in the grass and collects a bushel of leaves and twigs in his coat. We've given up trying to brush him off every time he walks in the house. As a result, there's so much yard debris on the floors, our living room needs raking. When the living room needs raking, it's safe to say the yard needs raking.

So after breakfast I head outside to the shed, and pull a rake from a tangle of bicycles and snow shovels.

It's a brilliant late-autumn day. The world is in Technicolor.

The dog sits in the front yard, his proud head turning from side to side, surveying his estate. His nostrils twitch excitedly as he savors the rich fall air.

I tune in to the football game, get a fresh cup of coffee and plan my raking strategy while I sit for a moment in the gentle, waning sun. The breeze has a trace of warmth to it, as if it is summer's final, dying breath.

As I sit there, I am aware that the yard is not getting raked. I fully intend to address that issue. But I need to sit and gather myself and listen to the game.

Okay. I'm up. I begin raking at the boulevard.

Our next-door neighbor, Lida, is taking her daily walk around the block. She's 98 but moves like she's 68. Despite the mild temperatures, she's dressed for an arctic expedition, with a parka hood pulled over her head and her eyes shielded from all light by a pair of oversized wrap-around sunglasses.

"Hello, Lida. Great day, isn't it?"

She gives me a startled, accusatory look. "How did you know my name?"

I'm slightly humbled that my dozen previous conversations with her during the past year have made no impression on her whatsoever.

I re-introduce myself and point out our house. But she doesn't seem convinced.

"You live there?" she says, looking at the house. "When did you move in?"

I feel as though I need to produce the title and deed to the property before she'll believe me.

"Well, I can't keep up with all the people moving in and out of that place," she says dismissively, referring to our home as if it were a crack house that should be condemned. With that, she continues on her way.

The woman from whom we bought our house lived there for 16 years. But to Lida, who moved into her home the week Pearl Harbor was attacked, I suppose that's a high turnover rate.

"Fumble!!!" I hear the announcer yell. I stop my raking and listen. "Let's see who has it…Illinois ball at the Gopher 38."

Damn. It's turning out to be a typical Gopher season.

I return to my raking. The thing about raking is, when you're doing it, you're generally not thinking about the actual act of raking. The mind wanders. And like most people these days, I've got bin Laden on the brain. Anthrax on my mind.

As I fill the plastic bags with leaves, I concoct schemes to catch the terrorists, and invent ways to secure the airlines and guard the water supply.

***

Another bag is ready to be taken out to the street. Down the sidewalk, Mr. Jimmy shuffles along chomping on an unlit cigar. He stops and says a few words with someone who's not there, then moves on, mumbling as he goes.

The dog bounds out to the sidewalk to greet him, tail wagging, tongue hanging.

I call the dog and ask Jimmy how he's doing today.

"Oh, okay, I guess," he says sadly. "Went to a funeral yesterday." He solemnly rubs his belly and studies the ground.

Matching his tone, I say, "Oh, I'm sorry to hear that. Who died?"

Jimmy looks at me as though I've posed a very interesting question. One he has not previously considered. "Hmmm," he says, scratching his unshaven chin. "I don't know."

Of course, Jimmy, who walks the neighborhood endlessly, from sunrise to sunset, just happened upon a funeral, and decided to stop in.

"I think he was a dentist or something," he says, straining to remember. "A man named O'Brien or Sullivan or something like that." Jimmy shakes his head slowly, grieving the loss of this Irish dentist, whoever he was.

He moves on, talking to himself, studying

the cracks in the sidewalk.

An anxious breeze stirs the trees, and the leaves fall like confetti. A car drives slowly past. For a moment, it looks as though it's traveling through a ticker-tape parade.

Throughout the neighborhood you can hear the sounds of fall: the rakes scratching the lawns, children splashing through piles of leaves, a football bouncing off the street. This movie-set world of America is one I will never take for granted again.

I return to the yard. As the bombs fall and the Ground Zero cleanup continues, I rake the leaves. It's all we can do. Just carry on with life. And perhaps, like Jimmy, mourn for people we never knew.

Dinner at the In-Laws

The moment we turn the corner, the dog knows where we are. His tail comes to life. He begins panting impatiently.

His head next to mine, he helps me navigate, bathing me in hot, anxious breath. "Not this house," he seems to say, "the next driveway, turn here, TURN HERE!!!" By the time I pull into my in-laws' driveway, he's ready to leap through the car window.

We open the front door to a chorus of "HellOOOoooOOOOs." There's an awkward head-fake moment as I attempt to hug my mother-in-law, Marjatta. I bump her glasses before figuring out which side my head goes on. As we embrace she pats me gently on the back, as if I'm some oversized infant she's attempting to burp.

From my father-in-law, Stan Sr., there's a hearty, no-frills Republican-style handshake. From Stan Jr., my brother-in-law, it's a casual guy-to-guy greeting. "Billeeeee. How's it going?" he growls.

Finally, I go to Linda's grandmother, who is seated in the corner next to her walker. They call her Mummo (pronounced moo-moo), which means grandmother in Finnish. Both she and Linda's mother are from the old country.

With surprising strength, the 86-year-old grabs my arm with both hands and eagerly yanks me down for a kiss. For an instant, she pulls me off balance, threatening to flip me head first over her walker.

"Hi, hi," she says, still gripping my arm. "Billeee, how's you mommy?"

"She's good," I say, loud enough to be heard next door.

"Dassa good," she says. "You say hi to you mommy for me."

With beers in hand, the men gravitate toward the football game on television. The voices of Pat Summerall and John Madden summon us like church bells calling the faithful.

It's a game of no consequence, yet we gather around the set as if the fate of the planet were at stake.

Like three ex-jocks in the broadcast booth,

we offer our expert analysis. "They have no running game," I say with great authority, reciting what I think I read or heard about this team someplace.

"They should have passed."

"Why didn't they call a time out?!" The opinions flow freely as we peel the labels from our beers.

Marjatta enters with a platter of appetizers, and Linda follows with napkins and plates. There's a hurried scramble to clear the coffee table to make room for the platter.

The men observe the scene in a football stupor. It slowly occurs to us that maybe we could help. But our half-hearted efforts to help are too late and we're told to sit and eat.

We settle onto the couch around the appetizers, our knees up to our chests.

Mummo sits in her chair across the way, looking at the television, but not watching it. I want to include her in the conversation. My mind races through my limited catalog of conversation starters with Finnish-speaking women over 80. Then I go with the old standby:

"Mummo, how was Bingo this week?"

"Who?"

"Bin-go. Did you play this week?"

She answers me but I'm not sure if she's speaking Finnish or English. Helpless, I look to

Linda's mother for translation.

"Mummo says that she didn't win this week but maybe next time she'll have better luck," Marjatta says.

I nod vigorously at Mummo through a mouthful of crackers and cheese, giving her the thumbs-up. That concludes our conversation.

As the game winds down and the appetizers dwindle, my brother-in-law sits on the couch, rubbing his stomach and flipping through the channels to find another game. His wife, Lynn, is in the corner discussing hair products with Linda. My father-in-law pours a glass of wine and proudly announces to no one in particular that he saved $1.67 per bottle by shopping at Sam's Club.

At my feet, the dog crawls under the coffee table, his tongue extended as he desperately reaches for a solitary fallen grape.

Finally, dinner is served. We are called to the table and take turns bumping into each other as we figure out where we are going to sit. After settling in my father-in-law leads us in grace.

"Oh Heavenly Father…"

There's a snort of repressed laughter from across the table. Out of the corner of my eye, I see my wife's shoulders shaking as she tries not to laugh. I kick her under the table. Despite the tough audience, Stan Sr. continues.

"We thank thee for thy bountiful blessings…"

For a guy who five minutes ago was ranting about greedy owners and overpaid athletes, his prayer is amazingly reverent and eloquent.

"Through Christ our Lord, Amen." The prayer ends and the passing begins. For the next five minutes, we are a conveyor belt of platters, bowls and baskets.

My mother-in-law directs activities from her end of the table. "Did everyone get the carrots? Stanley needs gravy."

Wine is poured and re-poured. The conversation grows louder and louder and my father-in-law roars with laughter as each member of the family gets roasted. He's jolly on wine and his hair is now standing up like he just got out of bed, or lost a wrestling match.

An hour into dinner, my mother-in-law makes her third lap around the table with dumplings.

"No, I couldn't. I'm stuffed."

"You sure you don't want to finish these? There's only two left."

She looks concerned that I'm not eating enough, and almost a little hurt. I can't say no. So I adjust in my seat and hope that somehow something inside me shifts to make room.

When I'm finished eating, I pull the oldest guy-trick in the world. With a great flourish, I begin to clear the table. My wife and her mother have put in six hours on this meal, yet my three minutes of work draws a near standing ovation from the in-laws.

After dessert, we sit around the table nearly comatose. Stan Jr. looks like he's had an overdose of codeine. I yawn so wide I almost dislocate my jaw and tears stream down my face. I give Linda a nudge as a signal it's time to go.

All of us help Mummo down the front steps and out to the car so Stan and Lynn can drive her home. The true danger is not Mummo falling, but that the five of us might trip over each other trying to help her.

I gather up the dog's stuff. Our coats are on, and we stand by the front door. Just as I reach for the door, Marjatta remembers. "You should take some leftovers." Tupperware is filled, and the warm plastic containers are added to the bag I carry.

We step out into the cold, and the air feels good. We get in the car, filled with the energy that comes from being with family, as though our batteries have been recharged.

Linda's parents stand on the front steps waving, as if they are sending us off on a voyage across the sea. My wife rolls down her window. There's another round of good-byes. That's forty-five good-byes according to my count. "Good-bye!!! Good-bye!!!"

To the dog she says, in a baby-talk voice,

"Chester, say good-bye to Grandma and Grandpa."
Oh, Lord, I think to myself, we need a child.

We pull away, and Linda's parents are silhouettes against the light from inside the house. They watch us drive off, and just before we disappear, they give us one last wave good-bye.

The Back of the Bus

Searching the house, I find my wife in the kitchen. I'm slightly breathless with my discovery. "Do you realize," I begin, slowly and dramatically, "that by riding the bus I pick up an hour and a half of productive time per day?"

She stares at me in disbelief.

"You know what that translates to per year?" I tap numbers into the calculator and show her the results.

"That's nine weeks a year!"

But it's not the figure on the calculator she can't believe. It's the fact that she's married to someone who is so hopelessly simple and dull.

I return excitedly to the calculator. "And you know how much money we save? Let's see, 36 miles a day, times 22 cents a mile, times 5 days a week times 50 weeks, I save—wow!!! Look at this!!!." But she has left the room, with the dog trailing behind her. Even he's bored.

I can't blame them. I am a recent convert to mass transit, having discovered the bus by accident a couple of months ago. And like someone who's just found religion, I am going through an obnoxious, proselytizing stage, preaching the benefits of the bus with a glassy-eyed conviction.

It all started when, due to uncooperative schedules and cars, I was rendered car-less for a day. As a last resort, I reluctantly boarded the bus for work, grumbling to myself, fully expecting the eighteen-mile ride to be an hour of stop-and-go, stomach-turning torture. Instead, I found the ride to be a relaxing time for reading and planning the day.

So now, here I sit on the couch as I do every morning, one eye on the newspaper, the other on the clock. At precisely 6:44 I grab my briefcase and head out the front door, walking the 239 steps (yes, sadly, I've counted them) to the bus stop.

Standing on the street corner, I dance stiffly from foot to foot, trying to keep warm against the cruel morning wind. I check my watch again. It's been less than a minute that I've been waiting but it seems much longer. Even time itself has succumbed to the cold.

Finally, salvation comes lumbering over the horizon. If I were a dog, my tail would be wagging. The bus glides to a stop with a hiss. I jump aboard and give the driver a grateful and runny nose, "Morning!"

As I make my way up the aisle, the bus takes off. Suddenly I'm transformed into a giant toddler who's just learned to walk. I stagger and lurch to the back of the bus and collapse into my usual seat in the middle of the back row. From here, I can observe everything.

I pull out my laptop, and blow into hands, which are still blue with cold. The bus pulls over and the Walkman kid gets on. He's a suburban teen trying desperately to look like he's from the city. He wears baggy jeans with the crotch sagging around the knees and a stocking cap pulled down almost over his eyes.

He sits down near me and stares sullenly and defiantly straight ahead. The music from his Walkman is a tin whisper. He's not happy to be here, and looks like a child who's forced to sit at the dinner table until he finishes his vegetables.

Next stop, we pick up the Bible reader. As he ambles down the aisle, his expression is dreamy, friendly and mellow, as if he's got a good scripture buzz on. He settles into his usual seat and digs into his knapsack, pulling out a dog-eared Bible. This morning he flips open to Paul.

I begin writing, but a bump in the road causes my first word to come out, "sgshlk," which doesn't really matter because I didn't have much of a thought anyway.

"Woweee, cold out there!"

I look up and see the chatty man boarding. "They say it's only gonna get worse," he says to the bus driver loud enough to be heard in the back of the bus. As he feeds the meter, he surveys the passengers, his voracious eyes searching for his next conversational victim.

Like students who don't want to be called upon by the professor, the passengers keep their eyes on their newspapers, trying to make it clear they're not available for conversation. But a businessman taking a sip from a mug of coffee is caught without defensive reading material. The chatty man swoops in on his prey, settling into the open seat beside him.

"Say, did you see *Survivor* last night?" the chatty man blares in a voice better suited for a public rally than a conversation. The businessman has no chance to answer.

"What a dumb show. I'll tell you what…" the bus accelerates and mercifully drowns out the sound of his voice. And when the bus comes to the next stop, he hasn't missed a beat.

"Yeah, so the systems guy at work says they'll have to reinstall the network software, and I says to him that's crazy because with our network application…" Then, rrrrrrrrrrrmmmm, the accelerating bus drowns him out again.

Miss America now makes her entrance. As she comes up the aisle, she leaves behind her a wake of subtly turned heads. Removing the purse from her shoulder she shakes her head and liberates hair that could star in a shampoo commercial. With her mane properly adjusted and cascading down the back of her seat, she turns her attention to her nails. Like a good book, they keep her absorbed the remainder of the trip.

I return to the blank screen of my computer. I've got a column due Monday and the anxiety is building in my stomach.

What can I write about? I've spent no time in a Mexican jail lately. I've not injured myself or met anyone famous or done anything exciting. Since I've started riding the bus to work, life has become pretty routine, with each day a near carbon copy of the next.

I can't face the dreaded emptiness of the page. Looking out the window at the passing rush hour I beg God for inspiration. Please give me something, anything to write about.

I look around me. The chatty man drones on. Miss America files a nail. The Walkman kid stares. I return to my computer, and slowly, the words begin to come.

Home Alone

M y wife is going to her girlfriend's cabin for the weekend. But the neighbors must think she's moving out. The car is packed with half the contents of the house.

She was supposed to leave by 8 a.m. and now it's almost 10. As she rushes out the door, there's a flurry of last-minute instructions and reminders. It's as if she's leaving a 12-year-old home alone for the first time.

"I put the number to the cabin on the kitchen counter. My cell phone is on if you need to reach me.

"Don't forget to feed the dog and make sure there's always water in his bowl."

"Okay. All right, no problem," I respond, nodding like a bobble-head doll.

"There are chicken breasts in the freezer and

plenty of vegetables and greens so you can make yourself a nice salad."

The car pulls away and the instructions are still being issued.

"And please keep the house clean. Remember we have guests coming to dinner Sunday night and I don't want to have to clean when I get home. Love you! Love you, Chester!!!!"

I wave good-bye until the car disappears around the corner. I turn to go inside, but Chester remains, staring in the direction of the car. After a few hopeful moments of looking at the silent street, he gives up and slinks in my direction, glancing up at me. "Bummer," he's thinking. "I'm stuck with you?"

The bachelor weekend has begun.

Within thirty minutes my buddy Eric arrives with his golf clubs. Wise-cracking as he enters the house, Eric heads straight to the refrigerator to help himself.

I rush to get ready for golf. As I approach the door, the dog lets out a heavy sigh of dejection and settles to the tile floor with a clump. He won't even look at me.

I try to explain to him that I'll be home soon, but he's in no mood to listen. Two farewells in a day is too much heartache for him to tolerate.

It's a perfect day and Eric and I go on a golf binge. Like a couple of happy drunks, we can't stop after eighteen holes. We deliriously order up another round of golf. By the time we finish the 36th hole of the day, it's getting dark.

We stop for dinner at a sports bar. While waiting to order, we gape at the giant TV screens with their endless parade of sports. Between innings of a ballgame, a dog food commercial appears and snaps me out of my trance. The dog!!! I've got to get home to let the dog out!!!

I rush home, fumbling for the keys at the front door. When I open the door, the dog is out of his mind with joy, skidding on the floor as he runs to his toy box to select a homecoming gift. He brings me a shiny wet squeaky toy. My tardiness is forgiven, no questions asked.

After going outside, he attacks his dinner with a life-and-death urgency. His tags rattle the side of the bowl as he ravenously devours his meal.

I grab a bag of chips, open a bottle of beer and settle in front of the TV. I own the clicker. I own the couch. I'm in bachelor heaven.

For dinner I open a can of soup and a jar of peanuts.

After the news, I lie on the couch in a TV stupor. I mindlessly flip through the channels of wasteland—a habit that drives my wife nuts—and observe the end of our civilization. Anna Nicole eats pizza in bed. Howard Stern asks his guest to remove her top. Cops handcuff a drunk, toothless woman in a trailer home.

It's well past midnight before I can gather the will to extinguish the blue light and head to bed.

Sunday morning I come downstairs and the house looks like the FBI executed a search warrant. Every cupboard and drawer touched yesterday remains open.

The kitchen screams of morning after. I'm greeted by a yawning, empty bag of Doritos with its last crumbs spilling out on the counter. There are beer bottles, cheese wrappers, dirty dishes, aluminum foil, soup cans, and a sink suffering from a severe case of constipation.

For breakfast I scavenge the kitchen like a raccoon in a dumpster. I find a jar of pickles in the refrigerator and a bag of croutons in the cupboard.

Sure, there's plenty of good wholesome food in the house, but all of these would require preparation. There might be slicing or measuring or thawing or mixing. All far too much work for me. If it can't be eaten directly out of the package, I won't bother.

By afternoon, I feel like I'm suffering from an overdose of processed food. A coffee mug now joins the living room clutter. The floor is carpeted with the Sunday paper and the TV is warm as a fever after five hours of political talk shows and sports.

I haven't bathed or shaved since Friday and I look like the guy on those Eraserhead T-shirts. As I simmer in my bachelor stew, the phone rings.

It's Linda. In contrast to my stale surroundings, her voice seems fresh and warm, like a sheet from the dryer. She announces that she's on her way home and hopes the house is cleaned. I assure her the place is spotless as I watch the dog eat a peanut from beneath the couch.

I hang up the phone and it's an immediate fire drill of frantic activity. The cleaning process reminds me of how I used to clean up after parties in high school before my parents got home.

Urgency creates efficiency, and by the time my wife walks in the door, I'm showered, shaved and the place is immaculate.

In the late afternoon, she goes to the garden to pick lettuce, basil and tomatoes. She turns on some music, pours a glass of wine, and with the dog at her feet, begins the patient process of preparing a meal.

I light the grill and she lights the candles. My time as a bachelor was fun for a while, but now I am thankful that beauty and civilization have returned to my life.

Home Improvement

The sound of a circular saw whines in the evening air. My neighbor is at it again.

As I struggle to light a match to start the barbecue, I watch in envy and awe as he works on the two-story, four-room addition he is building—by himself, in his spare time.

The Bible commands that we love our neighbor. But frankly, I hate my neighbor. He makes me look like an idiot.

I look around in shame at my home improvement efforts. Our backyard looks like the day after Woodstock. The grass is worn away from dog and foot traffic. All summer we've been sitting on a picnic table in the dirt. My solution to the problem has been to lay a couple of pieces of plywood over the dirt.

My neighbor raises the frame of another wall. Kachunk. Kachunk. He fires his nail gun, securing the framing, which now stands as a silhouette against the setting sun.

The truth is, we need a patio.

I take a swig of my beer and begin to ponder. If my neighbor can build a house with his own hands, why can't I build a measly little patio? I'm no Bob Vila. But it can't be that hard.

My wife comes outside. "How's the fire?"

"I think I'm going to build a patio," I proclaim with a steely and slightly inebriated conviction.

"Ooookay," she says, relighting the fire I've failed to keep going. Her tone is patronizingly skeptical, as if I just announced I want to become an astronaut when I grow up.

"No, I'm serious. Next weekend, I'm going to build a patio."

"I don't know," she says, heading back inside the house, "I've grown kind of fond of the plywood."

I give her a Jackie Gleason to-the-moon expression as she shuts the door behind her.

I stand and survey the yard, envisioning where my patio will stand. The notion of building something with my own hands seems exciting and even romantic. This patio will be my personal Hoover Dam, my Mount Rushmore.

All week, I have rock and gravel on the brain.

In the car I miss exits, at night I lay awake staring at the ceiling, in the shower I run out of hot water, all while contemplating how deep I should dig the hole, what type of stone to use, and how much gravel to order.

I visit three different landscape and stone places. I go to the library and get books on patios. I pick people's brains. I even trespass on private property to look at other people's patios.

On Saturday morning a truck pulls up and dumps six tons of rock, gravel and stone in front of the house. Our house is suddenly a construction zone. The eyes of the neighborhood are on me. The pressure is officially on.

In the back yard, I choose my spot. I jump on the shovel and break ground. The rich, cool earth opens, redolent and alive with healthy decay.

As I dig, the ground gives up clues to a mysterious past. I find an old 7-Up bottle, a dog bone from a distant decade, a broken flowerpot from some long-ago garden.

It feels good to dig, to work with my hands and be part of the earth. This mystical Walden Pond sensation lasts for about twenty minutes. Then the thrill is gone, and so is my back.

By afternoon I feel like I've been sentenced to hard labor in an Alabama prison. The hole I thought would take a couple of hours to dig is not even a quarter of the way done.

A parade of curious neighbors stops by. Everyone's a comedian:

"You burying bodies back there?"

"Let me guess. A mud-wrestling pit?"

The next morning I resume my digging and a light rain begins. The dirt is transformed into a sticky muck. It's as if I'm digging around in a giant pan of fudge brownies that stick to the shovel. By afternoon, the yard is a muddy war zone.

Six weeks later I'm lying in the hole I've dug, trying to level sand before laying the flagstone.

I look up and see Floyd, a neighbor from down the street, looking down at me as if I'm lying in my own grave. A retired city maintenance worker, Floyd is a sturdy old-timer whose German-Minnesota accent turns th's into d's.

"I see you're using dat flagstone over dere," he says gesturing to the two-ton stack awaiting me in the street.

"Well, you made a lotta work for yourself, I'll tell you dat. Dat flagstone is sooo uneven, you'll end up lifting and resedding every piece dree or four times."

"Yeah, well, we like the natural look of flagstone," I respond, hoping my explanation will end the conversation.

Floyd shakes his head. "I woulda gone wid da smood paver stone."

Floyd stands in silence watching me work for

the next five minutes, then, on bad hips, totters over to the house. With hands thick and gnarled from years of physical labor, he touches the side of the house.

"Looks like ya got some warping goin' on dere wid your siding. Might wanna replace dat 'fore it gets too bad."

I disingenuously thank him for his armchair advice and return my attention to the bubble on my level.

From the roof of his newly re-shingled addition, my neighbor waves brightly. "How's the project coming?"

"Super!" I lie. My mind fogged with doubt. The truth is I don't really know what I'm doing. But I continue on.

Fall is now about to turn to winter. Floyd was right of course. I've lifted and readjusted each of the forty-pound flagstone pieces four or five times. My quivering, aching back is fragile as crystal stemware. For the past couple weeks I've been popping Advils like M&Ms.

Moving as stiffly as the Tin Man, I place the final stone into the flagstone puzzle. I sweep sand into the gaps between the stones, and then, almost suddenly, the project is done.

"I'm impressed," my wife says as we settle into chairs on our patio. As the gloom of a late autumn evening descends, lights glow from inside my neighbor's addition.

"It was nothing," I boast, my chair rocking slightly on the uneven flagstone.

An icy wind provides a startling preview of winter, whipping leaves across the stone. My shivering wife scurries inside leaving me alone on my patio.

I sit alone in the cold, admiring my handiwork for a while. Then my attention turns toward the house, thinking of the siding that needs to be replaced.

As long as I'm at it, it wouldn't be that big a deal to take down that wall and extend the kitchen out this direction. I mean, really, how hard could that be?

Spaciness – The Final Frontier

In the kitchen, I ponder the big question: "Why am I here?"

I was just in the living room. Now I am in here. What am I looking for? While I think about it, I check out what's in the refrigerator.

At the kitchen counter I eat a piece of cold, leftover pizza and scan the newspaper.

On the obituary page, there's an Anderson age 89, a Hanson age 92, and a Johnson age 79. Near the bottom, a younger face jumps off the page.

Age 46. My age. Yikes.

I study the notice and it dawns on me: I went to high school with this guy! I vaguely remember Jack from sophomore year gym class—a skinny kid with wild hair who, if I recall correctly, threw up after the mile run.

"Of a heart attack, survived by wife..." reads the notice.

Wait a second. Guys my age aren't supposed to die of heart attacks. Drug overdose, suicide, car accident, fine. But a heart attack?

Now I remember. Car keys. That's what I'm looking for.

I stomp around the house, frustrated. What could have happened to the keys?

I yell up the stairs in a voice that is half whining and half accusatory, demanding that my wife tell me where she has hidden the keys.

"Earth to Mr. Spacey," she calls down, with a certain delight in her tone. "Look out the window."

Outside, the car is spewing a cloud of exhaust into the freezing air. Oh, that's right, I forgot. I started the car ten minutes ago to warm it up. I say good-bye and head out on my errands.

The door rings as I walk behind a bundle of shirts into the drycleaner. I toss the heap upon the counter and start counting shirts.

As I count I wonder: Was Jack overweight? Maybe he was a smoker.

A girl saunters in from the back of the store, and in one motion, grabs a green order form and a pen, and collapses against the counter.

"Phone number?" she says absently.

She is pretty, pierced and wears the bored

expression of a teenager on the clock. Low riding jeans cling tenuously to a jutted, tattooed hip. With a puff of her lips, she blows a wisp of hair from her face.

"Um, ah," I stammer, as if I'm trying to recall the words to the Gettysburg Address.

Her pen hovers impatiently above the order form as I search my mind for my home phone number. Thanks to speed dial, I never dial home anymore.

After taking my order, she heads back to retrieve my cleaned shirts and I think about Jack some more.

What if he was in great shape? What if he died on an exercise bicycle at the health club? That would really be depressing.

I pay for the shirts, and head out the door. As the bell rings, I hear the girl calling me. "Your shirts. Hello!!! You forgot your shirts!!!"

I head down the street to retrieve my car from the parking lot.

The parking attendant is bundled bravely against the bright, fierce cold. Despite the brittle day, he is as jolly as a Packers fan tailgating outside Lambeau Field in January.

I hand him the parking ticket.

"Parking is $5," he says between sniffles. "Towing is another $45."

"What?!"

"Sorry buddy. You forgot to leave your keys in the car. We had to tow it out of the way to park cars."

Aw man. I'm so spacey these days. I need to tie strings on my fingers and set alarms and make notes to myself just to get through daily life.

I follow the attendant to the pay booth. Inside the cramped space, I blow on cold fingers before writing the check. In the corner, Judge Judy is on a little black-and-white TV with a coat hanger antenna. She is scolding a litigant and I feel like she's talking to me.

"Your car is over there," the attendant says, pointing a mitten to the corner of the lot. "There's a black Infinity in front of you. I'll move it out of your way."

"A black infinity in front me?" The words of the lot attendant haunt me as I make my way out of the lot into the city traffic.

Is that what follows life? A black infinity? Or is there something more? Jack knows the answer. And so does everyone else who's passed before us.

At the stoplight I look up. The buildings are brilliant against the liquid blue sky. Great white billows of exhaust rise from their tops like cumulous clouds on a summer's day.

The rolling white against the infinite blue reminds me of the day the Challenger went down. I remember Reagan quoting that poem that night—about how the astronauts had "slipped the surly bonds of earth, to touch the face of God."

A black infinity? Or touching the face of God?

The car behind me honks. Back on earth, the light has turned green and I didn't even notice.

Horncroft Acres

The decade of the 1950s is a black-and-white photo in my mind. That's when we lived in the "old neighborhood" in Minneapolis. There, the houses were old, the trees brooding and ancient, the sidewalks cracked and gray, and the neighbors cranky and elderly.

Then, in June of 1961, my parents announced to the six of us kids, that we were moving to a new house in the suburbs.

"A diner? Why are we moving to a diner?" My five-year-old mind whirled with the possibilities of living above a restaurant.

"No ya' goof," my older brother gently informed me. "EDINA. We're moving to Edina."

Edina at the dawn of the '60s. The moment the moving van pulled up to the house, it was as if someone flicked the switch, and the world turned to living color. All was suddenly new and young and promising. The houses were modern, the neighbors were young and friendly, and the yards spacious and green.

Even the country had a new, young president and the state had two new ball teams. Everything was now possible and within reach.

Unlike the old dark Tudor-style house we left back on Russell Avenue, our new house was sprawling and different from anything I'd ever seen. There were bedrooms in the basement. And a room for us to play I pronounced the "moozement room" that had a bar and a sink and a shuffle board game built into the tile floor.

The garage door was electric. There were huge closets to hide in, woods in the backyard, and a creek nearby.

My friends and I roamed the neighborhood, unsupervised. We were constantly endeavoring to set something on fire, to blow things up. We built tree forts, and traps, and rafts for the creek. And in the streets there were ballgames.

Now, forty-two years after moving into Edina, my mother has sold the house. I come back to the old homestead.

I go up into the attic to grab the boxes of junk I've been promising my mom I'd go through since

1979. With a new family about to move in, I can't very well keep up the same line of BS about how I'll come over one of these weekends to get rid of the stuff.

In the attic I open the musty old boxes. There's a picture of me from the late '70s. I almost forgot I had a mustache back then. It's not a good look. The mustache, along with my curly, bushy hair, gives me the shady, unctuous look of a '70s-era porn star.

Beneath the yearbooks and old love letters and the Kodak prints that now stick together and need to be peeled apart, I find the hardened, curled notebooks with my old writings and journals. It's embarrassing stuff: the oh-so-earnest introspections of a college freshman. I don't want anyone to ever see this stuff.

I grab the collapsing boxes and head downstairs and make one last tour of the house.

Most of the furniture is gone now. As I walk through the house, my footsteps produce a hollow, melancholy echo.

Though nearly empty, each room is alive with memories. In the den, I can hear my parents' friends at a cocktail party. The peels of laughter rising along with the cigarette smoke. The manly voices of the men. "Robert. Gimme a scotch," they'd growl. "Just a splash of water."

In the living room there were the Christmas

mornings. The wild, gift-opening frenzies among the piles of wrapping paper. Toys raised up triumphantly. "Look what I got!"

In this bedroom I remember jumping off the top bunk onto my little sister's bed and bouncing across the room—behavior that was strictly forbidden, and therefore, all that much more fun.

The kitchen table, where politics, sports and religion were discussed—everyone speaking at the same time. After dinner, my dad insisting we say the Rosary. And me, rolling my eyes and complaining the entire time. "Dad, It's sooo repetitious," I'd whine. "Didn't God hear us the first time?"

There was no possibility of my parents moving out of this house when my dad was alive. This great house—which he gave the tongue-in-cheek nickname of "Horncroft Acres"—was his baby. Everyone thought he was insane back in 1961 to have bought such a house.

A salesman with no salary, living on 100 percent commissions, with a house full of kids to support. He sold things like toilet bowl deodorizers, ironing board covers, salad bowls, playing cards, coffee cups, mops, and any other type of line he could land. My mother would lie awake at night, wondering how they could possibly afford house payments of nearly $200 a month.

But he was always doing crazy things. Like

when he signed up to have refugees from Poland live with our family for three years, without telling my mom until the day they arrived. Or when he and my mom took in two foster children from Vietnam after the rest of us had moved out.

But he knew everything would work out. And somehow it always did.

I step out the door and strangely, feel no sadness. My mom—who just turned 80—will have her own place for the first time in her life. She's as excited as a college kid getting her first apartment. Another chapter begins.

I load the boxes and get in the car. As I sit there, I can see my dad, limping down the driveway on sports-battered knees. He always walked everyone out to the car. He's joking and keeping up a baseball diamond line of chatter and encouragement as I back down the driveway. "Good luck, kid. Lotta pep. Talk it up. Loads of prayers."

As I drive away I swear I can still see him. He stands at the end of the driveway waving. I'm halfway down the street before he turns and shuffles his way back to the house.

Sod Almighty

His shorts reveal winter-white legs. On his feet are sandals and black socks pulled up to his knees. He wears a stopwatch around his neck and headphones in his ears.

My father-in-law has just finished mowing the lawn—for the second time this week. Today was a diagonal day. Next time he'll mow crosswise. The alternating pattern gives his yard the checkerboard look of the infield of Yankee Stadium.

The sidewalk, driveway, and the entire length of the curb have been edged with a surgical precision. The sheer neatness of the place makes you want to snap to attention and salute.

Stan walks across the green blanket of lawn and suddenly stops. He looks around as if he's hearing the voice of God. Standing still he listens.

The Twins have just scored in the bottom of the eighth, his Walkman tells him. He resumes his business.

He turns on the sprinkler, which hisses and spits before sending its streams cascading across the lawn. Stan studies his stopwatch through bifocals and sets the timer for exactly twenty-two minutes, which he has determined to be the optimal watering time for each section of the grass.

While my wife and I regularly poke fun at him for his garden attire and his stopwatch, the truth is we've got lawn envy.

Our yard is in terrible shape. It has more bald spots than a thirty-year class reunion. Mowing produces no satisfaction, only clouds of dust. And when it rains, there's mud. The dog leaves paw prints on the carpet that look like he walked on an inkpad before entering the house.

We need a new lawn. Being a man afflicted with the I-can-do-it-myself disease, I decide, despite my wife's advice, to take on the project myself and not hire it out.

How tough can laying sod be? Green side up is all I have to remember. I'll whip off the project in a few hours.

I ask a friend if he would help me.

"Sure," he says. "Don't do it! Hire somebody! There, I just helped you."

I didn't really need him anyway. I know I can do the job myself because of the magic of the rental store. There I rent enough equipment to start a landscaping business.

First, I rent a sod cutter to cut up the old grass. Then I rent a machine called a Dingo—a sort of walk-behind Bobcat. The plan is to scoop up the old sod with the Dingo and dump it in a trailer.

I haul the two-ton Dingo to my house. I start it up and practice in the street by scooping up a pile of dirt.

It's like playing Tonka Trucks—but for adults. Scoop, turn, drive, dump. Hey, I'm digging the Dingo! This is fun! Now to take it up onto the lawn for some real work.

At the rental store, I asked the guy if the Dingo could go up curbs. "It can climb a wall," he assured me. I don't doubt him. The Dingo has wheel treads like an army tank.

The Dingo aggressively climbs up the curb, but it keeps climbing and does a wheelie, landing on its back. The wheels spin uselessly in the air. The machine begins bleeding oil and gas. The engine sputters, chokes, and then dies after an explosive bang that sounds like a pipe bomb going off.

A dense, black, oily cloud rises from the machine and slowly drifts across my yard. My wife and neighbors emerge from their houses expecting to see body parts in the trees. Their startled expressions soon turn to curiosity, as they comprehend my predicament.

I have a machine heavier than a car tipped on its back like a helpless beetle.

Another fine mess. I'm an idiot! What a disaster! Perhaps I've bitten off more than I can chew this time.

But in a rare stroke of engineering genius—perhaps one of two moments in my entire life—I put old bricks under the treads, hang on the shovel, and tip the machine up just enough so it can catch some traction. Miraculously I get the Dingo up on the lawn.

On the lawn I soon discover I have the same type of control over the shovel as an infant has over its hands. I lower the shovel with a boom. I move the Dingo forward and instead of scraping off the top layer of old sod, it digs two feet into the wet earth.

The Dingo turns on a dime, but in the process twists and spools the grass into a muddy mess. After an hour of experimenting with the Dingo, the yard has turned into a giant mud pie.

The next morning, the mud has dried. The old sod is encased under the hardened muck. How am I ever going to get rid of all the old grass? I am buried in depression. What have I done?

Then I remember the one person I can call in a

situation like this. The God of Sod. Stan the Man.

He shows up for work an hour later in work clothes that make him look like an escapee from a chain gang. But I'm too depressed and thankful to make fun of his outfit.

He surveys the damaged yard like a Red Cross relief worker arriving on the scene of a disaster. He is not bothered by the enormity of the task. With the patience of Job, he begins pulling pieces of sod out of the muck. He cleans the excess dirt off each piece with the same care with which he cleans bottles and cans before putting them in the recycling.

The next day my wife joins her father in the work party. Then my mother-in-law arrives to help, and finally my sister. Two and a half days later, I lay down the final roll of sod. On my knees, I look up to heaven in thanks.

For the next three weeks we nearly drain the town's water tower keeping the lawn wet. Finally, the big day arrives. I get to mow the grass for the first time.

That evening, Linda's parents stop by. Stan and I stand in the yard and talk while Linda and her mom go inside. When they leave, my wife excitedly asks what we talked about.

I tell her we spoke about garden hose connectors, weed wackers, how high to set the lawn mower, baseball and the stock market.

She shakes her head. "Boys," she says, walking into the house.

Perhaps she was hoping to hear that we had hugged and wept and shared feelings. Who knows?

I drag the hose across the lawn and turn on the water. For a brief, vain moment I look around deeply satisfied. The grass is flawless, green as spinach. I watch to see that the sprinkler is properly positioned. Then, looking at my watch, I set the timer for exactly twenty-two minutes.

The Card

I t's nearly 5 p.m. on Valentine's Day. I'm in the grocery store, standing in the card aisle. I stare at the rack. Frozen. Baffled.

I've looked at two-dozen cards and each one is dumber than the last. Panic sets in.

An amazingly bland version of "Hey Jude" is being pumped through the store like stale air-conditioning. I can't concentrate. The clock is ticking.

I am somewhat relieved that I am not here alone. Two other men, looking sheepish and desperate, lurk among the racks of cards like patrons of an adult bookstore.

We are the brotherhood of the clueless, the great procrastinators. If Valentine's Day is the

Super Bowl of love, we are the Lions. We aren't even in the ball game.

Cards, gifts and notes—they're not my strong suit.

This year, my excuse is as lame as the cards left on these picked-over racks. My wife told me that because we went overboard for Christmas, we shouldn't get anything for each other this Valentine's Day. So I took her at her word and didn't get her anything.

Then, at the 12th hour, it occurred to me that "not getting her anything" does not mean, literally, "not getting her anything." After all, this is Valentine's Day.

I pick another card from the rack. On the front is a misty photo of a rose. "To my darling wife," it says, in swirling script. The poem inside sounds like it was written by a frustrated English major. Discouraged, I put it back.

Frankly, I don't get this whole greeting card business. People pump their own gas, prepare their own taxes and remodel their own bathrooms. Yet, when it comes to the expression of their most intimate feelings, they outsource the project to Hallmark.

Maybe I should write my wife a letter instead. I think about my parents during World War II. They met just before my dad was shipped overseas. They carried on a four-year courtship through letters. Now that was romantic.

But I'm no good at letter writing. I'm not even a good note-jotter.

When I send a thank-you note, it has all the sparkle and personality of an IRS notice.

"Dear So-and-So,

Thank you very much for the whatever. I had a great time. It was great to see you. Thanks again."

I wish I could dash off brilliant, witty, heartfelt notes. The kind they used to send in the old days.

But these thoughts are not helping me in selecting a card.

I check my watch and drift over to the "humorous" Valentine's section. There I look through cards featuring bad puns, frogs, bag ladies and puppies. Nothing is remotely funny. My theory holds up: Anything labeled "humorous" is guaranteed not to be funny.

It's not that I don't appreciate and love my wife. I just wish that love didn't need to be expressed by the act of shopping.

Shopping makes me clammy. A timer goes off in my head when I walk into a store. After fifteen minutes, I start to feel restless. After a half hour, I feel faint.

Why can't love be expressed with some other activity, like rotating the tires or reconciling a bank statement? Not that I love doing these things, but at least I'm not a complete incompetent.

But shopping for cards and gifts and all this, well, it's like asking me to play the lead in *Grease*. I'm just not well suited to the task.

My wife, on the other hand, is an expert. Say it's my mother's birthday. Linda will travel to four different stores to find the exact type of hand soap my mom once mentioned she liked six months ago.

Then she'll wrap the gift like a work of art, complete with sprigs of herbs or some such thing tied up with satin ribbons.

She'll find the perfect card, write a beautiful little message, and then, two minutes before giving the gift to my mom, she'll hand me a pen, hold open the card and say, "sign here."

I scrawl four simple letters—B i l l—and that's the extent of my contribution to the effort. Aside from the love and companionship, this off-loading of the card and gift-giving function may be the single biggest benefit of marriage.

I pick up another card.

There's a picture of two teddy bears cuddling on the front. "To my sweet wife," it says. Inside, it reads,

Snuggling up close
or cuddling tight,

Saying good morning
or kissing good night—
Wherever we are
or whatever we do,
I'm happy just being
married to you.

It's got to be the corniest card I've seen. But maybe it's because I'm so desperate and pressed for time that this sappy and insipid card strikes a chord with me. I decide to go with it.

I stop by the flower section and pick up the last of the sad bouquets.

I hurry home. Fortunately my wife is not home yet. I sit down in my office to sign the card.

"To my sweet wife," I write. Damn. Mistake number one: I've plagiarized the wording from the front of the card. I continue:

In heartfelt prose, I write, "You are the best wife a guy could in the world." Oh no! A typo.

I attempt to fix the mistake with lines and arrows and cross outs. I've created a mess.

My handwriting is like that of a second grader. The printed letters have the uneven jumbled look of a ransom note. The lines float upward, I miscalculate space. I need to squeeze text in along the margins.

"Love you more and more each day!!!" I write, throwing in extra exclamation points to compensate for the sheer banality of my message.

I stuff the withering flowers in a jar of water, and I place them, along with the card, at the center of the dining room table. I dim the lights so that the flowers don't look half bad. Inspiration strikes, and I light a candle.

Two minutes later, my wife walks in the door loaded with bags from Target. She stops. Even though it's Valentine's Day, she looks surprised that flowers and a card are awaiting her.

After the bags are unloaded, we pour a glass of champagne (which she bought) and sit down. She opens the card and reads the stupid poem. Then she reads my message to her.

She needs to turn the card sideways to decipher my tiny, scrawling, trailing message of love. As she reads, a smile crosses her face, her eyes glisten, and all I can think is that I wish I'd done more.

A Dog's Life

Whenwe pull up in front of our house there's a head in the bay window. While my wife gathers her things from the car, I make my way up the front walk. The urgently attentive figure in the window watches my every move. As I near the door, I rattle the keys. The head in the window tilts in a question mark, then disappears.

When I turn the key there is an explosion of canine excitement. He bursts through the door and charges past me like it's open seating at a Who concert.

"Hello, Chester..." I say to the empty air.

By the time the words leave my lips, he is airborne off the front steps, and sprinting down the walk toward Linda.

She screams for him to stop. But he is ninety-five pounds of delirious happiness, and has all the control of a semi that's lost its brakes. He barrels into her, nearly knocking her over. He joyfully slobbers on her pant leg, breathlessly grateful for her long-awaited return (we've been gone nearly an hour and a half).

Then, as if he's just remembered that he left something boiling on the stove, he rushes back into the house. A moment later he reemerges, this time with a toy duck stuffed in his mouth.

"Oh, thank you, Chester…" I say. But again he runs past me like I'm invisible.

Wheezing through his nose, he circles Linda, showing off the gift he has brought her. He settles down next to her, leaning against her leg. Like a smitten schoolboy, he gazes up at her adoringly, pining with puppy love.

Meanwhile, I stand at the front door feeling like a backup singer for Beyoncé—utterly ignored.

It is only when I grab a ball that he notices my existence. This is our chance to bond. I throw the ball down the sidewalk and he sprints after it. He overruns his target and his claws scrape the sidewalk as he clumsily applies the brakes.

But after a couple of tosses, he becomes distracted. "Where is Linda?" he wonders. Staring at the house, his jaw slackens and the ball drops. He races inside and in a panic, searches the house.

I am left standing alone. The Rodney Dangerfield of dog owners. I get no respect.

He finds her in the kitchen preparing his dinner. He stands by her side, watching intently. He smacks his jowls and anxiously tap dances back and forth in anticipation. Before it even touches the floor, he has his head in the bowl. Dinner lasts all of thirty seconds as he gobbles down his crunchy cereal.

After three rawhide treats, he follows Linda up to bed. He sleeps on the floor on her side of the bed. The carpet is stained by his black oily coat, leaving the shadow of his image, like a sort of Shroud of Turin. My side of the bed remains spotless.

In the morning, he is spread eagled on his back. With his paws in the air it looks like rigor mortis has set in. Like my wife, he never, ever gets up in the night. I watch the two of them sleeping for a moment, then start my day alone.

Now it is seven years later. Chester is 12 years old. Or 84 in dog years.

We open the front door. Chester wakes with a start and struggles to lift his sixty-pound frame off the floor. After a brief greeting during which his tail swings languidly a couple of times, he settles back down on the marble floor with a boney clunk.

A short while later he wants to go outside. I

open the back door and he saunters lazily out into the snowy night. He sniffs the night air a couple of times, looks back at me, then disappears into the darkness.

Around dinnertime, I smell something good in the kitchen. There's ground beef sizzling in the pan. Hmmm? What are we having tonight? Sloppy Joes? Spaghetti? I reach in the pan to grab a piece of meat.

"Ah, ah," my wife scolds. "That's for Chester." Wow. It's come to this: I'm not allowed to eat the dog's food.

I go outside and call Chester for dinner. But there is no sign of him. I listen but the only sound I hear is the falling snow. I call again. Nothing. Finally I whistle, and a snowy lump in the yard slowly rises and shakes off.

The old man slowly ambles inside where his warm meal awaits. He impassively regards his dinner, offering only a half-hearted nibble out of politeness to the cook. With a sigh, he lies down again, resuming his life as a breathing throw rug.

At night, when we go upstairs to bed, he doesn't follow us, but instead settles in on the floor at the bottom of the stairs. Only if he absolutely has to will he climb the steep steps to our bedroom.

At 3 in the morning, I hear him clumping up the stairs, huffing and puffing like a locomotive going up a mountain. I pull the covers over my head hoping he won't see me.

I was already up at 1 to let him out. Twice a night, every night, he needs to go out.

He knows better than to try to wake my wife. If sleeping were an Olympic event, she'd own several gold medals. So he stands on my side of the bed and pants, torturing me with breath that smells like tuna gone bad.

I need sleeeeep!!!!! Please go away!!!

But he persists and I give up. I can't take it anymore. I angrily throw the covers back, grumbling and stumbling as I make my way through the darkness.

I open the back door. A wall of frigid air greets me. It has stopped snowing and the sky has cleared. A full moon illuminates the night. The shadows of the trees are crisp and blue upon the fresh fallen snow.

I watch the ancient silhouetted figure plod his way along the upper yard, sniffing and inspecting. He stops and raises a leg, looking around as if checking for hidden cameras.

Shivering with cold, and impatient with fatigue, I hiss at the dog to hurry up and come in.

He bounds towards me, and for a moment he seems young again. He jogs into the house and heads to his water bowl. I shut the door and turn off the light, listening to the familiar rhythm of his lap lap lap, slurp slurp, lap lap lap.

Before I head up the stairs, he comes to me. I'm dying to get back into bed. But he seems insistent we spend a moment together. So I stop and give him a perfunctory rub beneath the jowls.

His fur is still cool from the outdoors. As I scratch he lifts his proud head. I check the clock upon the wall. Oh brother, look at the time. I finish petting him but he still stares at me with his wise old eyes. It's as if he wants to tell me, before he goes, that he loves me too.

Dude, Where's My Bike?

Most everyone has one—an old, lonely, unused bicycle that sits in the garage or shed behind the lawnmower and the snow shovels. That's where my trusty old, indestructible Schwinn Le Tour rests. Even though its spokes are laced with spider webs and the chain is rusty, I know I could plant myself on its cruel leather seat and it would run just fine. But after nearly thirty years of service, it's time to give this bike to charity, and look for a new bike.

So on my way home from work I stop off at the bike shop. Looking around, I see there are more ponytails and sandals in here than a Greenpeace convention. None of the sales staff looks like they own a fossil-fuel-burning vehicle, which is exactly how you want the people selling you a bike to look.

A kid with a nose ring steps out from behind the counter to help me.

"Yes, I'm looking for a bike," I say stupidly. Standing there, with my briefcase in hand, I suddenly feel as square as a member of the Nixon cabinet.

"Cool," the clerk says, his head bobbing slowly. "Mountain or road, dude?"

"Aw, yes, uh road, I think." The last time I shopped for a bike there were 10-speed racers and stingrays and that was about it.

"Cool," the head bobs appreciatively again, as if I've just said something profound. "Lemme show you what we've got, man."

I follow the ponytail back among the bikes. The clerk pulls a bike out of the rack and lifts it with one hand.

"Check this out, man. Light as a feather," he says, in a voice that sounds like he's just taken a hit of pot.

I lift the bike and simultaneously check the price tag. Sure enough, light as a feather but expensive as a diamond.

I eventually settle on a more reasonably priced bike. But by the time they finish upselling me on accessories—water bottle holder, speedometer, light, rack, toe clips, bike lock, bell—the bike is as expensive as a mortgage payment. But that's okay. As long as I ride it once in a while.

I take my new bike on a Lewis and Clark expedition of discovery to see where the bike path near our house goes. To my amazement, I find that it is possible to ride twenty miles from our house to downtown, and stay on a bike path nearly the entire way.

This is fabulous. I could bike to work! Think of the money I could save, and the shape I could be in! Thus begins my latest midlife obsession.

Now I'm a bike-to-work infomercial. I can't stop talking about it. I can take any conversation and eventually steer it back to the fact that I bike to work.

"BORING!" my wife says to me with her hands over her ears as I describe to her in excruciating detail my ride home.

Even my poor mother-in-law, who is interested in just about everything, is bored to paralysis when I describe to her how the LRT trail hooks up with the Kenilworth Trail near Cedar Lake.

And then, there's the bell on my bike. My wife has a field day making fun of me and my bell. I'll admit, it's not the most macho feature, and it does make me sound like I'm selling ice cream. But what she doesn't understand is that you can only yell "On your left!" so many times on a forty-mile bike ride. And when you're traveling twenty miles an hour, and you approach a gaggle of elderly women out for their morning walk, and you yell "on your left," they tend to panic, and run into each other, lurching one way then the other, like indecisive squirrels on the road.

Only the gentle ding ding of my bell is capable of alerting them that I'm approaching from behind without sending them into a confused state of panic.

Dawn is breaking, and I'm riding the path to work along Lake Minnetonka. Those successful, striving few, who've made it here to the water's edge, emerge from their castles for a morning jog.

There's the Pamela Anderson look alike, deadly serious about her running, carefully exhaling through pursed red lips. And a red-faced man who shuffles along bent in the middle as if there's a knife stuck in his belly.

Up ahead are the warm-up suit ladies. They march briskly, swinging and pumping their arms, their conversation animated and bright as the morning. They smile at me, and as I peddle past, I can hear their nylon suits go swish, swish, swish.

I look down at my speedometer. I push a button and it tells me how far I've gone. I push another button and I can see my average speed. This is fascinating. I push another button and look up just in time to see the deer.

Holy !@#%!!! I slam on the brakes and hop off the bike, my heart pumping.

The deer stands in the middle of the path, posing like a high-priced model.

Why is she not moving? Is she going to charge? If she chose to, this powerful animal could kick my butt into oblivion. I know I shouldn't be afraid of a deer, but I can feel the hair on the back of my neck rise.

"Hello, deer," I say in the most non-threatening voice I can muster.

The deer ignores me and looks around as if I'm the least interesting thing in the woods this morning.

Suddenly, she bounds off into the woods. Then out of nowhere, four more deer come leaping across the path. Each looks like Randy Moss going up for a pass over the middle. The graceful powerful athletes are thrilling to watch. I wait for a moment to be sure the coast is clear, and then hop back on the bike to resume my journey.

Forty-five minutes later I reach the bridge over Highway 100. Below me the highway is a parking lot of rush-hour frustration. The drivers in their cars stare blankly ahead, resigned to the wait. Through the open car windows I can hear the woofer-rattling baritone voice of Tom Barnard on the radio.

A couple miles up the path, I pass under the

394 bridge. The great freeway roars a few feet above my head. A homeless man sits next to a fence under the freeway and rubs his eyes against the morning light.

I ride through the Walker sculpture garden, past the cherry spoon, over the footbridge and into Loring Park. In what other city in America is such a ride possible?

In the park I encounter foot commuters and the first sense of downtown urgency. There's a woman in a business suit and tennis shoes, walking quickly with her headphones and steaming cup of Dunn Brothers coffee. A man scoots along in a perfect gait, as if balancing an apple on his head.

I make my way through downtown. In the bike lanes I feel like a sitting duck among the oblivious drivers and the hulking buses. I finally arrive. I park and lock my bike in a rack across the street from my building.

It feels good to get off the bike. I'm pumped and ready for the day.

In the evening after work, I look forward to my ride home. When I return to the rack, I stare dumbfounded at the empty place where my bike used to be. I search again. Am I so absent-minded I forgot where I parked my bike? No, it was here.

I look around. Every person on the street is suddenly a suspect. I am angry, depressed. I feel stupid and violated. There's a thief out there ringing my bell and I want him in prison.

But then I think about the menu of life problems one could have, and I realize this is nothing. It's just a bike. I can always get another bike. My head bobs slowly. A new bike. Cool.

A Shady Character

We've just moved into a new house. At closing, the sellers gave us a check for $1,200 for the removal of the dead oak in the backyard.

Two days after we move in, my wife calls me at the office. There's a guy named Ray at the front door who runs a tree service. He says he can take down the tree for only $800 and that he's fully insured and licensed.

"Great! Let's hire him," I tell her.

"I don't know. I don't have a good feeling about this guy," my wife whispers into the phone.

"Honey, what could go wrong—it's just a tree? And $400 is $400."

The next day, I race home to meet Ray and his crew at 2 as he promised. By 6, I've left Ray four messages wondering where he is. Ray is a no-show.

Serves me right. I should have listened to my wife.

A week later, my wife again calls me at the office. Ray and his crew are at the door, waiting to start the job.

"What? Put Ray on the phone," I say. I'm ready to chew him out, but Ray preempts me.

"Hello, Mister Wha-ite?" Ray says in an amiable drawl. "Mister Wha-ite, I DO apolo-GIZE for any inconvenience I caused last week?" His voice rises at the end of each sentence as if he's asking a question.

I find myself disarmed by his aw-shucks delivery. And when he explains that he didn't show up for the job because he was in a car accident that put him in the hospital, I'm the one who's nearly apologizing.

Feeling sorry for him, I give him another chance. I tell him to wait until I get home so I can see his proof of insurance, before starting the job.

My wife gets back on the line, and again in sotto voce says, "I'm telling you, I don't have a good feeling about this guy."

"Honey, trust me, OKAY?"

When I arrive home I am surprised to hear the whining of a chainsaw from the backyard. I'm not sure if I'm more annoyed that he didn't wait until my arrival, or impressed that he is so anxious to get started.

I walk around to the backyard. It looks like a juvenile detention center. None of the crew on the ground is old enough to have a driver's license. A couple of the kids are kickboxing with each other. Another smokes a cigarette and stares into space. And a pudgy kid who looks like Pugsley from the Addams Family is sitting on the edge of a flowerpot, his butt bending the petunias.

"Where's Ray?" I ask the kid with the cigarette.

"Awww. Ray?" he says, rubbing his eyes as if he just woke up from a nap. "Yeah…Ray, he went to bid another job. He'll be right back."

"Jesus H Christ!!! What da hell are you boys doin' down dere?" A voice booms out from the branches above.

Up in the oak, a big panda bear of a man stands on a limb forty feet up. He wears a fishing hat with the front brim turned up like Crazy Guggenheim, and a pair of bib overalls, and apparently, nothing else. The nipples of his big beefy chest play peek-a-boo out the sides of the overalls. He gestures wildly at the boys with a chainsaw in one hand while holding onto the tree with the other.

"Grab dat goddam rope dere," he says in an accent that is pure Fargo.

"Not dat rope for Chrissakes!!!" He bellows in a voice that can be heard throughout the neighborhood. "Dee odder one!!!" The two kickboxers bump into each other trying to heed the tangled orders from above.

Up above, the chainsaw growls and spits wood chips. A limb slowly tumbles through the branches, crashing precariously close to the neighbor's fence. The man in the tree spots me shielding my eyes against the sun, watching him with concern.

"Doncha worry, Mister. I know what I'm doin'. I seen a guy do dis yesterday."

I force an unenthusiastic laugh and point at the guy, acknowledging his joke. He is joking, right?

"Hey Mister, do you have anything to drink?" asks Pugsley. "Maybe like Coke, or Pepsi?"

The thought bubble above my head reads: "Who do I look like, June Cleaver?"

But I smile and serve the boys their drinks as they make themselves comfortable sitting on our patio furniture. I'm starting to lose my patience. "Where's Ray?" I'm wondering as I march inside and avoid eye contact with my wife.

A half hour later the chainsaw is quiet. I look out the kitchen window. The boys are still reclining in the patio furniture, blowing smoke rings in the air.

The man has come down from the tree and is opening a can of Old Milwaukee. The branches on the oak are gone, but the main trunk remains standing. I storm out the door.

"What's going on here?" I ask the man, pointing at his beer and the lounging crew.

He smells of sweat and gasoline and wood chips. Though I'm only five feet away, he addresses me as if I'm standing down the block.

"Oh, yeah," he yells, taking a swig of beer and wiping his mouth. "I'm done for da day."

"What do you mean done? The tree is still standing?"

He shrugs. "Ain't nothin' else I can do. We need the big saw to cut down the tree but nobody here can get the damn ding started 'cept Ray." He gestures toward Pugsley who's pulling furiously on the starter rope of a saw big enough to fell a Redwood. "We gotta wait for da boss to finish da job."

After a dozen tries, Pugsley grows frustrated with his toy and tosses the saw onto the grass. The blade gouges the earth leaving a large, black-dirt divot upon the lawn.

I rush inside. Steam is rising from my ears as I dial Ray's number.

Ray answers and I can hear the sounds of happy hour in the background. His words come stumbling out like drunks leaving a bar. "Misser Wha-ite? Is 'ere a problem of some sort?"

"Yeah there's a problem, Ray," I say, my voice

crackling with anger. "Your crew is sitting around flicking cigarette butts onto the lawn. The guy in charge is opening his second can of beer. And did I mention: the oak tree is still standing?"

"Misser Waahite. You haffa unnerstand that ah am a bizness man and ah wanchu pletely satis-fied wiss da job. I'll be right over in five minutes to finish the job myself. And I do apolo-GIZE."

Three hours later. No sign of Ray. I've left him nearly a dozen messages. I step out the front door. The crickets have begun their chant. The boys lie in the front yard looking up at the stars. The man in the overalls is crawling inside the mouth of the wood chipper, trying to dislodge a stuck limb. "God---- son of f---- b---ing thing," his voice echoes throughout the quiet neighborhood.

At 10:30 I hear voices in the front yard. I go outside to see what's happening. A silhouette staggers out of the darkness and shakes my hand. Ray's hands are rough as dried mud and his grip has a menacing strength to it. The smell of stale booze lingers in the air as Ray blathers on, effusive with apologies and promises. He won't shut up until I mention how good he looks considering the car accident and all. This stops him cold. He has no idea what I'm talking about.

Three days later, the job is finally done. Sort of. The yard is a mess and we've paid Ray off. But his truck and wood chipper remain in front of the house leaking oil onto the street. I've left him repeated phone messages to move his truck. None of them have been answered.

I call the police. Turns out the truck belongs to Ray's girlfriend. The tabs are expired and her license has been revoked. As I watch the towtruck drive off, I leave Ray a message informing him of the truck's departure. Thirty seconds later, my cell phone rings. I look at the number. Ray has finally called me back. I do not bother to answer. I click the phone shut and look at my wife.

She doesn't say a word. She doesn't need to.

Continuing Education

The bell rings. Recess is over. We are told to stand quietly in straight lines on the playground before reentering the school. But who can stand still? I'm restless. Bored. I want to stir things up.

To get attention, I do an impersonation of Sister Mary Grace, our elderly fifth grade teacher.

My classmates egg me on. Richard Garrity, Dave White and Tom Frey are laughing when suddenly their eyes rise up behind me, and their faces darken as if clouds have passed in front of the sun.

I turn to see what they're looking at, but a hand grabs me by the back of the neck. The vice-like grip belongs to the feared Mr. Toppel, the Heinrich Himmler of the school. The paralyzing effect of the hold is immediate and absolute. It is the 1960s version of today's Taser.

He raises me by the scruff like a mother cat lifting a kitten.

"So, White, you think you're pretty funny, don't you?"

This, of course, is one of those questions for which there is no appropriate answer, even if I weren't flopping like a walleye on a stringer.

"Eeekkkggaaah," is all I can manage in response.

Fortunately, he spots misconduct further up the line. He discards me like yesterday's newspaper, and marches off to administer another session of corporeal punishment.

This is but one of a hundred memories of my grade school days. In eight years of Catholic grade school, I was a Cal Ripken of sorts—setting a record for the most consecutive days of getting into trouble.

In ninth grade I am sent to a Catholic military academy for further straightening up, but this doesn't help. I can't stand the saluting and dressing in a uniform that makes me look like a mailman. In 1970, nothing could be less cool.

The following summer, I spend two months begging and pleading with my parents to pleee-aaase let me go to the public school. My father finally gives in, as long as I promise to attend daily Mass and say the Rosary the rest of my life (a promise he never held me to, but never let me forget).

The public school is intoxicating. There are girls in short skirts, and guys with long hair. For the first time in my life, I don't wear a uniform to school. And best of all, discipline is lax. I take full advantage.

By the time senior year rolls along, I've done a grand total of about twelve minutes of homework. I have an attendance record even the Alabama National Guard wouldn't tolerate.

All I care about is sports and partying and being with friends. I have no interest in learning. That is, until Everett Anderson's English Literature class.

***

He tells us to listen to the words. Listen to the language. Listen to how Shakespeare paints the picture…

"To-morrow, and to-morrow, and to-morrow, Creeps in this petty pace from day to day"

He is a tiny man, a little over five feet tall, but he fills the room with a booming, musical voice. He jumps up on a desk, and continues:

"Out, out, brief candle! Life's but a walking shadow, a poor player that struts and frets his hour upon the stage and then is heard no more."

He jumps off the desk landing light as a bird, and makes his way down the aisle. His voice softens dramatically, "What does this mean to you to 'strut and fret' upon the stage?"

The bell rings, breaking the trance. We collectively groan as we pack up our stuff and leave the magic of his classroom.

At the door, he talks to each of us as we pass, offering words of praise and encouragement.

"Remember, Come what come may, time and the hour run through the roughest day."

"William," he says to me, "that essay you wrote was wonderful."

"Huh? It was?"

"You have a gift. Use it! You can do whatever you want."

This is the first time I've heard such a thing from a teacher.

***

It's our 25th high school reunion. With my wife in tow, I wade through a sea of middle-age; a smile of semi-recognition is frozen upon my face as I say hello to the name tags, and then the faces.

In the corner, I spot Everett talking to a group of his old students. We make our way over to him. He is his same brilliant self, gushing over the adults we've become. I introduce him to my wife, and the two of them get along instantly, gossiping like girlfriends.

He must be in his 70s now, but he looks great; almost the same as he did twenty-five years ago.

I ask him how he's doing.

"Well," he says, matter-of-factly, "I am dying. I have inoperable cancer." Then he adds merrily, "But I'm taking my medications, and I feel fine most days and I cherish each and every day." It's as if he's about to jump up and click his heels.

His ebullience in the face of death leaves me speechless. I know that anything I say in this situation will sound banal and insipid. He sees my loss for words, and changes the focus.

"But you. Look at you! And your wife—I love her! She's wonderful. I'm so happy for you."

Leaving the reunion, I resolve to send him a note to tell him what an impact he made on me, and to thank him for being the teacher he was.

But each day my good intention is superseded by the urgent and important things of life, none of which I can now recall. And two years later, when I read in the newspaper that Everett has passed away, the note remains on some forgotten to-do list. I kick myself.

"Tomorrow, and tomorrow, and tomorrow," the words from long ago come back to me.

Hair Today, Gone Tomorrow

My wife walks in the door with her hair four inches shorter and three shades lighter than when I saw her last. And even though she told me twice this morning that she was going to get a haircut, I don't notice a thing.

She looks at me. "Well? What do you think?"

"About what?" I reply dimly.

She sighs and rolls her eyes. "This," she says, pointing at her head.

I stare blankly for a moment, before it registers. "Hey, you got a haircut!" I announce proudly.

"Brilliant deduction, Sherlock. What do you think? Stephen talked me into it. He wanted to try something different."

Stephen is the hairdresser she's been seeing since before she even knew me. She is devoted to this man. But as far as I can tell, it's a one-sided relationship.

It takes about six weeks to get in to see Stephen (and God forbid you should try to cancel) and for the privilege of sitting in his chair, it costs the equivalent of a luxury car payment.

Stephen loves to experiment with my wife's hair. And all the while he's clipping and teasing and foiling and whatever else he does, he unloads his latest round of boyfriend problems on her like she's Dear Abby.

"He thought it would be fun to try it shorter. Do you like it?" she asks, studying my face for a reaction.

Wow, I'm thinking. What the hell was Stephen trying to do here? Her hair looks like Courtney Love the morning after. I could have done better with a can of mousse and an egg beater. I hate it.

This puts me in a delicate, precarious position. I feel like one of those guys who's been called in to defuse a bomb. I need to be oh so careful.

"Umm," I say, buying time to compose my response.

"I like it," I say weakly, my voice rising at the end of the sentence in a forced sort of way. But she picks up on the falsetto of fabrication.

"You hate it."

"NoooOO," I say desperately, my voice still an octave above believability.

"I thought you'd like it."

"I do. In fact I love it," I say, lying like a tobacco executive. "I just, I…I…I…need to get used to it, I mean, it's so…so, DIFFerent."

Her lower lip curls up in a pout. She slumps into a chair. "I hate it too. What am I going to do?"

***

When I get a haircut, it's a different story.

On my way home from getting an oil change, I stop in to one of those chain discount haircut places stuck in the middle of a strip mall.

I walk in and the door goes bling. A toddler in the waiting area breaks away from his mother and nearly takes my knee out. The air is filled with the sweet cloying smell of hair chemicals and the whirring sounds of blow dryers.

Behind the counter a teenager whose eyes are darkened with too much make-up is sweeping hair into a pile. She sets down the broom and comes up to the register reciting a greeting straight out of corporate headquarters.

"Welcome to Quick Clips. What can we do for you today?"

It pains me to have to answer this painfully obvious question. "Ah, I'd like a haircut?"

"Phone number?"

The girl's fingernails claw the keyboard. My record comes up.

"Okay…" she bends down to read the screen, her gum cracking. "Bill?!!"

"That would be me."

She giggles. "Okay, Bill, take a seat, it will be just a few minutes."

On the table in the waiting area is a heap of tired old magazines. I scrounge through the tattered copies of *Redbook, Glamour* and *Good Housekeeping.* I finally grab a six-month-old issue of *People* and settle back into my plastic chair for the wait.

From behind the magazine I scout the stylists. Here it's a game of roulette that determines who will cut your hair. Will it be the chubby girl with the purple hair and nose ring? Or the gabby blonde? Maybe the Asian woman in the corner?

I return to my *People* and read old news about Brad and Jennifer.

"Bill? Bill!?"

The woman at the counter has just come back from break. She greets me in a husky voice made rough by a lifetime of smoking, and as she leads me back to her chair, she lets out a productive cough.

She's of indeterminate age, somewhere north of 40, but too old to be wearing skin-tight Lycra pants and a top that reveals far too much cleavage for the occasion.

I sit down in the chair and try to spark some small talk, but this goes nowhere. She fastens a paper collar around my neck that is just tight enough to raise the veins in my neck ever so slightly. I look in the mirror. Draped in the cape, I am just a head seated in the chair. Feeling claustrophobic, I fight to bring my hands out from under the cape so I can read my magazine.

She grabs the hair above my ears and pulls it straight out like Bozo the Clown. Her hands still carry the smell of her cigarette break.

"Take it off above the ears?" she asks, talking to me in the mirror. She looks tired and distracted. Her hair is frightened into a crunchy perm and when she reaches for her scissors, I catch a glimpse of a tattoo on her tummy.

She sprays my head with water and begins cutting. She is quick and rough and as she cuts, she picks up on an earlier conversation with the stylist next door, complaining about a rotten boyfriend, a teenage daughter she can't control and a car that needs repairs.

The snip snip snip of the scissors comes perilously close to my ears. The comb dragged through my hair feels like a thatch rake. Hair tumbles into the valley of my magazine so that I have to brush it aside to read.

In just five minutes, the ordeal is ended. I look up, stunned by what I see. I haven't had hair this short since the ninth grade, when I was sent to military academy for a year.

I pay my $15 and decline the offer to "purchase product." Outside in the parking lot, my head feels defenseless against the frigid air.

When I walk in the front door I quickly learn what my wife thinks about my haircut.

She snaps to attention and salutes me. "At ease, soldier! Wow! That's short!"

The next morning, I sit up in bed and my wife begins to sing the jingle to the Chia Pet commercials.

"Chi-chi-chi-Chia!"

I drag myself out of bed and look in the mirror. The hair that's left stands straight up. She's right. I'm a human Chia Pet.

My wife joins me at the mirror. She too is still suffering from the effects of her haircut. Her hair looks like it was put in a blender and set to frappe. Winter has drained the color from our faces. We stand there and make fun of ourselves in the mirror. And happily, this too will pass.

The Visit

It's a flawless, sunny Sunday afternoon, a perfect day to be anywhere but here at the nursing home.

My wife and I pull into the circular drive that is set beneath hovering oak trees. We drive by the front entry, where residents are being picked up and dropped off.

On the radio, it's the Vikings and Packers. Brett Favre scrambles and throws to the corner of the end zone. Touchdown Packers. The score is tied.

I punch the steering wheel. "Sonnofa…I'm telling you this defense stinks!" A woman loading her elderly mother into the car thinks I'm yelling at her. She gives me a horrified, shocked look. I smile and wave, trying to communicate that it's our secondary I'm yelling at, not her.

"There's a parking spot at the end," my wife says.

I absently pull into the space, lecturing my wife on football as I maneuver the car.

"I'm telling you, you cannot win without defense. Bud Grant knew that. And how can you win with turnovers and penalties?" But I might as well be talking to her about bauxite extraction processes. She has no interest whatsoever.

"We're late. I hate being late," she says, looking at her watch.

I wait until the last possible moment to turn the car off, leaning toward the radio listening to the kick-off.

"C'mon, my parents are already here. They're waiting for us," my wife says, already out the door.

We walk in the front entry and the automatic doors groan as they slowly open. The doors stay open long after we pass through.

"I can't believe I forgot to set the recorder for the game," I grumble as we pass through the lobby. In the air lingers the soft-food-and-bed-pan smell of a rest home.

We pass a man asleep in a wheelchair, his chin on his chest. The treads of his tennis shoes are still virginal from non-use.

"Maybe I can find a TV here someplace."

"I think we go to the third floor," my wife says.

We go up to the third floor lounge and spot

Mummo sitting with Linda's parents. I wonder if she'll recognize me.

As we approach the table, the look of recognition slowly crosses the 90-year-old's face. "Billeee!" she cries out to me, greeting me as if I'm the second coming.

I kiss the paper-thin skin of her cheek and sit down at the table. In front of her sits a beige tray with the picked-at remnants of her afternoon meal.

She pats my wrist. "Tank you now for coming. You work today?"

"No, Mummo," Linda shouts. "It's Sunday."

"You GOOT boy for coming," she says. "I luff you."

There is absolutely nothing I have done to deserve Mummo's enthusiastic and undying luff. My visits here are as frequent as solar eclipses, yet they always elicit her effusive thanks.

Linda's mother, on the other hand, spends long and patient hours here nearly every day. Yet when she arrives home from a visit, the phone will be ringing and it's Mummo wondering why she never comes to see her.

"How tsunami?" Mummo says.

I look at my wife, puzzled. "How's your mommy?" Linda translates.

"Oh, she's great. Very good," I say, finally catching on.

"You say 'hi' to you mommy for me."

"Yes, yes. I will," I say, nodding my head vigorously.

There is a lull in the conversation. I look around wondering if the game is on anywhere.

In the corner of the lounge a television with bad reception blares with the noise of a cop show from the '80s. The screams and gunshots and squealing tires create a weird audio juxtaposition with the serene elevator music being piped into the room. In front of the TV sits a woman hunched over a game of solitaire, her back to the set.

I return my attention to the table and wonder aloud what the score of the game is. Linda's father sits up. "Yeah, it must be the fourth quarter by now." He nods in the direction of the solitaire player. "Hey, why don't you ask her if we can check the score?"

I turn and look at the woman. Her face frowns in concentration as she turns the cards. She seems oblivious to the violence on the TV behind her.

He eggs me on. "C'mon, Billeeee."

I can't resist his challenge. The family watches as I walk over to the card player. With the hat-in-hand deference of the scarecrow approaching the great and powerful Oz, I ask the woman if maybe we could change channels for a moment to check the score of the football game.

The woman's head snaps up and she glares

at me. It's as if I've insulted her family, her god and country all in one sentence.

"I was listening to the program!!!" she growls, perturbed by the outrageousness of my request. On the screen behind her, two men trying to strangle each other crash through a window.

"Sorry, sorry," I say, quickly back-peddling away, like I've accidentally stepped into the women's restroom. I return to the table.

Linda's father is thoroughly amused. "Looks like you've made yourself a new friend," he says. Everyone has a good laugh at my expense. Mummo, sensing something funny has happened, laughs too. She pats my hand again. "You look GOOT today."

After an hour or so, it's time to take Mummo back to her room. Programmed not to waste, she grabs the salt and sugar packets from the tray and stuffs them in her bag.

I push her chair through the lounge, steering through an obstacle course of walkers and chairs. The hallways are decorated like a preschool, with happy posters and ornaments touting the upcoming holidays.

We roll past white-haired souls, bent like question marks in their chairs. Some sleep. Others mutter to themselves. Each room we pass is a snapshot of infirmity. A gray-faced man with an oxygen tank stares at the ceiling. A woman angrily shouts out. Finally, we arrive at Mummo's room.

An embroidered pillow that says "Grandmothers are special" sits on her bed. On the wall are family pictures. There's Mummo and her late husband, squinting in the sun, standing tall and proud in front of their Ashtabula, Ohio, home. And down here are bouffant hairdo snapshots from the '60s, and some plaid wide-tie photos of the '70s.

It's been a long journey to this place for Mummo. A refugee of war, she fled Finland with her children when the Russians invaded. They went first to Canada, then to Ohio and now she's finally come here to be close to her daughter.

We say good-bye to Mummo and she grips my arm like she's clinging to a life raft. "You behave, Mummo."

In the lobby I spot a television with a football game on. But the game doesn't matter to me anymore. Linda and I walk out the door into the cold bright air. There is a lightness in my step I didn't have when we arrived here. I breathe deeply, happy to be walking free.

Chester

The sun is high and hot on this Fourth of July afternoon and the air is soaked with humidity. We are attending a pool party at a friend's house and our dog is with us. Despite the heat, Chester refuses to go in the water, or even to sit in the shade. For him it is far more important to stay at my wife's side than it is to be comfortable.

So there he sits at Linda's side, lying on a pool deck that is heating up like a stovetop. His thick black coat is hot to the touch. With his tongue spilling out the side of his mouth, he pants like he's just run a four-minute mile.

Since she can't coax him in the water, Linda tries pouring water on his steamy head. But he shies away as if the water were poison.

In all the time we've had him, I've never

once seen him go near water, much less swim. In fact, we have our doubts that he can swim. It seems strange that a dog that is a retriever and Newfoundland mix would have such a fear of water.

I watch him panting in the heat and shake my head.

"Chester, you're just a pathetic momma's boy, you know that?" He ignores my ridicule and looks adoringly at Linda. I set down my drink and sprint for the pool. I dive into the deep end and the water is barely cooler than the air. I swim toward the drain and as I do so, I hear a splash above. Someone has joined me for a swim.

When I clear the surface I'm shocked by what I see. A frantic Chester paddles in my direction. He's come to save me! He swims his nose up to mine. "You okay?" he seems to ask.

Realizing that I'm all right, I see his brain shift gears. "Oh, shit. Got to get out of the water! Got to save my own ass!!!" With his paws pumping and his nose snorting, he slowly turns and heads to the side of the pool near the diving board. As he paddles, he looks like a woman going for a swim who doesn't want to ruin her hairdo.

He gets to the wall and starts to panic when he can't climb out. I swim beneath him and attempt to push his big wet bottom onto the deck. But the soaked 100-pound dog feels like a bag of cement and it doesn't help that I'm inhaling water because I'm laughing so hard.

By this time, half the party is in the rescue act, and we finally hoist the frantic dog onto the deck. Soaking wet, he looks like a giant black rodent and he seems genuinely embarrassed to be seen this way. He gives a powerful shake and a mist rains upon the screaming, scattering bikinied women. His coat is now a mass of ringlets.

The reluctant star ignores the applause and adulation from the appreciative audience. All he cares about is finding Linda, who throws her arms around the wet dog as if he's a war hero who's returned home.

"Such a good boy! Did you save your daddy?"

His dripping tail fans like a windshield wiper set on high. He looks up at Linda, pleased that she's pleased. With his mouth hanging open, I could swear he's smiling.

The phone rings and snaps me out of my trance. It's Jim. He's on his way. He'll be at our house in ten minutes.

A combination of butterflies and heartache gnaw at my gut.

I look out the front window. Linda lies in the grass with Chester. He sniffs the young spring air. Nearby, the first flowers of the season are bursting through the ground.

This will not be easy.

Chester has always been the perfect Zen-dog. He's never growled or barked at anyone. Every stranger is his immediate, long-lost friend. We never had to tie him up because he'd never leave the yard, except when he'd occasionally saunter across the street to greet a neighbor.

Big dogs would threaten him, little dogs would nip at him, but Chester would never fight or retaliate. His tail would continue to wag as he turned the other jowl.

I go outside and tell Linda that Jim is on his way. I know I've got to be strong. We exhort Chester to come in the house. "C'mon, boy. Get up. It's time to go in."

He regards us with tired old eyes. Finally he makes the effort. Like a wounded fighter trying to get up off the mat, he struggles to his feet, but falls to the ground. Linda and I need to help him up.

We lift his bony body and extend his legs like we're setting up a card table. Wobbling and staggering, he makes his way into the house, following Linda. Inside he flops down, exhausted, and falls asleep in his favorite spot at the foot of the stairs.

We sit and wait for Jim.

Nothing can be said to make it easier. But it helps to remember.

"Remember how he'd chase rabbits in the yard? What was he thinking? It was like a cement truck trying to catch a Ferrari."

"And how we used to sneak him in the offices of Law & Politics, and the time he peed right in the lobby? And remember him in the mornings…"

The doorbell rings. Our good friend Jim is here. He's been Chester's vet for years. Chester should recognize his voice, but he doesn't lift his head or even open his eyes to greet him. He's just too tired. Everything is too much work now.

And so he ignores Jim and the fuss being made over him, and the tears, and even the needle as it enters his front paw. He just wants to sleep.

The passage is peaceful, and almost imperceptible. The gentle rising and falling of his belly finally ceases. And just like that, our friend, our child, the constant fixture in our marriage, is gone.

We kiss and pet him one last time. Loyalty, love, patience and courage. Could it be God gave us dogs to teach us something about how to live?

The Surprise

Sixty-five friends and family members have arranged sitters and carpools and have journeyed through the Friday evening rush hour to be at our house exactly at 7, for the surprise.

It is now 8:15 and the crowd stands huddled in the gasoline fume darkness of our garage, clutching their drinks, waiting for the signal.

Outside, I stand in the driveway, next to my wheelbarrow. Wearing muddy jeans and a T-shirt, I pretend to be doing yard work.

My cell phone rings. It's my sister, Katie. "We're turning off highway 7, we'll be there in two minutes," she says in a deadpan, covert agent voice.

She and my sister Jean and sister-in-law Sarah have taken my wife, Linda, out for happy hour to celebrate her 40th birthday, which is coming in two weeks. Now they are driving in a caravan back to the house, supposedly so that Sarah, who has not yet seen our new house, can see the place.

I snap the phone shut and give Cindy the signal. I've assigned her the thankless task of directing and maintaining order over the crowd.

I hear her give the two-minute warning, announcing to the group that everyone has to be quiet. But they ignore her like she's a substitute teacher.

Everyone, it seems, is now a comedian. Through the garage door I hear the wisecracks from Tom and Eric and the grunts and snorts of suppressed laughter, the contagious kind that breaks out at funerals.

"You're standing on my foot!!!!!!! Where's the bathroom in here?? Can I get another beer?"

Like a method actor getting into character, I take a shovel full of dirt and place it into the wheelbarrow.

Up the street I see Linda's car turn the corner, followed by my sisters.

"She's here!" I yell at the door.

The garage door is alive with noise. "SSSHHHHHHHHH!!!! SHUTUP!!!!!" The cocktailing crowd tries to silence itself in voices loud enough to be heard across the street.

It will be a miracle if we can pull this off.

Linda pulls into the driveway. I begin my

performance of nonchalance nothing-going-on-except-me-working-in-the yard act. I force a little small talk with my sisters, and then attempt to coax Linda to step to the garage door.

"I can't seem to get the garage door open. I press the code and it doesn't open. Give it a try and see if you can make it work."

Linda looks at me like I'm an idiot. "What do you mean you can't get it open?" she says as she marches for the control pad. Suddenly, she stops short and looks at me like she knows something is going on. I give the signal and the door flies open so fast it nearly runs off the track.

SURPRISE!!!!!

Linda turns her back on the crowd, overwhelmed with shock, and starts walking away. When she turns back around and realizes the size of the crowd, there are tears in her eyes.

She sees her parents, who had told her they were going out of town for the weekend. Others in the crowd whom she hasn't seen in a year step forward to hug her.

We take her to the backyard. For the first time in weeks, the rain has stopped and the sun now slants through the trees. The fresh mowed grass is a glowing, flawless green that makes you want to pick up a wedge and chip golf balls.

On the lawn are chairs and tables with white linens and bud vase centerpieces filled with fresh flowers. A banquet table is teeming with hors d'oeuvres: There are wedges of cheese I can't pronounce nestled among grapes and fancy crackers.

Shrimp arranged like synchronized swimmers are spread across a silver platter. In tin buckets on the patio are bottles of wine and beer buried to the neck in ice. The whole scene looks like a wedding reception.

Linda gathers it all in and looks at me, astonished. As if on cue, a couple of her friends come up to me and gush with praise. "BW, the hors d'oeuvres are fantastic!" says Barbara.

"And the scented candles in the bathroom. What a nice touch!" says Kathy. I modestly accept and bask in their praise.

The party is a complete success. I'm getting all the credit, yet I haven't done any of the work.

How did I do it? How did I, a person with the culinary skills of Curly Howard and the work ethic of Maynard G. Krebs, pull off this event? Here, for the first time, I reveal the secrets: The Lazy Man's Guide to Party and Event Planning.

Cleaning and Preparing the House

Twenty-four hours before the party and I haven't lifted a finger to clean the house. I'm sitting on the couch watching TV as Linda vacuums around my feet.

You see, Linda is the type of person who will clean the house if the guy from the gas company is coming to check the furnace. Because she thinks Sarah and my sisters are coming over to see the house Friday night, she's been on a two-day cleaning spree. As I flip through the channels, I rest assured knowing the house will be spotless.

Food

The trick here is to let the culinarily gifted people around you know how utterly clueless and helpless you are.

A week before the party I say to my mother-in-law, "Do you think people will need anything to eat while they wait for the surprise? Maybe I should get some chips or something."

She can't resist coming to my rescue. "I could make a few appetizers for the guests to nipple on," she says in her Finnish accent.

"Really? You're sure it wouldn't be too much trouble?" I ask with the sincerity of a time-share salesman.

Of course, her offer of "a little something to nibble on" becomes an elaborate spread of hors d'oeuvres.

At work, Cindy is the party planner of the office. I tell her my plan to feed the crowd. "I was

thinking of getting some frozen lasagnas and popping them in the oven after Linda leaves the house."

Before I know it, she's on the phone with
her neighbor Gus, who owns Christos Greek
restaurant, to have him cater the event. While
the two of them plan the menu, I sit with my
feet on my desk, checking the American League
box scores.

Seating

The thought never crosses my mind that
sixty-five people might need a place to sit while
eating dinner. At work Cindy asks me what I'm
going to do about tables and chairs. I repeat the
words with a question mark: "Tables? Chairs?"

This propels Cindy into action. She calls a
dozen friends who are coming to the party and
has each bring a table, chairs and a centerpiece.
Problem solved.

Dishes and Place Settings

This required actual effort on my part. I had
to drive over to my in-laws house to approve
place settings.

My mother-in-law drags me into the basement
to show me the silverware she is wrapping in
napkins.

"I thought the yellow napkins would be pretty with these plates. Do you think that would be okay?"

"Hmmm," I say, scratching my chin and pretending to study the situation. I'm thinking about who I could get to fill out the foursome I have booked for golf on Saturday.

"You know, I think…"

My mother-in-law leans forward in anticipation of my verdict.

"I think the yellow will work just fine." She is relieved that I approve.

Booze

Because the party is at our house, I can't store all the beverages at our house. So I outsource this to my father-in-law, who hauls several cases of wine and beer to the house, plus the coolers and ice. When he arrives, I offer assistance by directing him where to put everything.

The Toast

After dinner, I stand on top of a cooler and propose a toast to my wife. Even here, I get assistance from Henny Youngman.

"My credit card was stolen the other day and I've decided not to report it. The thief is spending less than my wife.

"Communication is important. If you want your wife to listen to every word you have to say, just talk in your sleep.

"But seriously folks…" I raise a bottle of beer to my wife, and for a millisecond, sincerity creeps into my voice.

"To the best thing in my life."

Though it is sappy and simplistic, it is heartfelt. And unlike the food and the candles and the flowers, this one's from me.

Something to Chew On

It's another e-mail from my wife. I know what it is even before I open it.

"Isn't he cute?" the message says.

I roll my eyes and click on the attachment. A black puppy with oversized paws that look like they've been dipped in white paint stares at the camera. His big earnest eyes and slightly tilted head seem to plead, "Won't you adopt me?"

Why does she do this to me? I've told her I don't want a puppy.

I read the story beneath the picture: Fletcher is an eight-week-old Labrador-Newfoundland mix. Born in the pound, he was scheduled to be euthanized when an outfit called Canine Castaways rescued him. Now they are trying to find a home for him.

I have to admit, he is a good-looking pup. But

we have other priorities in our lives right now and our schedules would not allow it. If we were to get another dog, I'd want an older, house-trained dog. That's the sensible thing to do.

I reply to the e-mail, "We're not getting a puppy!!!"

Having laid down the law, I assume that's the end of it. But Linda persists. The e-mails keep coming. She can't stay away from these Web sites. It's her Internet porn.

It's a quiet, beautiful late Sunday afternoon in August. I'm in the porch reading the paper. Maybe I'll go for a jog this afternoon. Or perhaps a bike ride. Or maybe I'll hit some golf balls. Ah, the luxury of freedom and spare time.

The phone rings. After several minutes, Linda appears at the porch door, with a guilty look on her face.

"Remember the puppy with the white paws from a few weeks ago?" she says, looking at the floor. "Well…he's coming over to meet us in ten minutes."

"What?"

"That was the woman from Canine Castaways on the phone. He was adopted a week ago but the family returned him because he and the cat didn't get along. I just thought we could meet him. Maybe this was meant to be."

Pleading like a schoolgirl, she says,

"Pleeeeeaaase?"

Caught off guard in a moment of weakness, I stammer, "But, but, I thought we agreed no puppies…And, well…oh, I, suppose it can't hurt just to meet him."

A few minutes later, the doorbell rings. In jogs the puppy with paws as big as slippers.

He frantically weaves a figure-eight between our legs, tying us up with his leash. He flops on his back for some petting, his pink tongue hanging deliriously out the side of his mouth. After a minute, he gets up to explore, his long tail thwapping walls and doors as he zigs and zags his way through the house.

In the backyard, he romps about, chasing his tail and tipping himself over. It's all very cute.

After five minutes of frenetic activity, he lies down on the back steps, resting his nose upon his front paws. He falls asleep with a sigh, and breathes the high-pitch snore of a sleeping puppy. It's as if he knows he's auditioning for the part of the lovable puppy.

I look at Fletcher, and then at Linda watching him. Linda is practically lactating with motherly love. She mouths the words so as not to wake him, "Isn't he A-DOR-ABLE?!!!"

I'm toast. I should have known. Never, ever look at a puppy. They are not like cars or houses or TVs. You can't comparison shop. You meet a puppy and it's all over.

"Annie and Cindy say we'll just love having a puppy," she says, attempting to close the sale.

I know that if I say no, it will not end the battle, only prolong it.

"OK," I sigh, shaking my head and casting my eyes heavenward. "Let's keep him." Linda is stunned. She throws her arms around me and scoops up the puppy, smothering him with kisses.

After writing a check to the Canine Castaways and saying good-bye to the woman, we look at each other. Reality sets in.

We don't have food, or toys, or treats, or a kennel. And what we really lack is knowledge about training a puppy.

We rush to Petsmart, arriving minutes before it closes. We run through the store, shopping like Paris Hilton, buying anything and everything the employees suggest.

Thus begins the puppy odyssey—the low-grade torture of having each moment of each day consumed by this pooping, peeing, chewing, mischief-making machine. Life becomes an adventure.

I can't take a shower without him whining and scratching at the bathroom door. So I put him in the kennel. In the shower I can hear him yelping and crying, protesting the sheer injustice of being left alone for ten minutes.

I hurry my shower, barely rinsing off the soap. He's still barking and howling when I step out. I wrap a towel around myself to see what the commotion is about.

When I walk in the room where the kennel is, I'm hit with a wall of odor. He's pooped in the kennel and it's all over everything.

I open the door of the crate and carefully remove the blanket, trying hard not to spill anything. With my hands occupied, he snatches my towel, leaving me vulnerable in ways I don't need to explain.

Fearful he will mistake my newly exposed anatomy for a chew toy, I drop the blanket and prepare to defend myself.

"Down boy!!! Down!!! Stay away! Damn it, go chew the curtain! Anything!"

Productivity plummets. The most routine of tasks now become an arduous struggle. I can't tie a shoe without him tugging at the laces. When I do the dishes, Fletcher tries to crawl into the dishwasher and lick the plates. If I sit and read the paper, he barks at me. If I continue to ignore him, he tries to eat the paper or bite my toes.

He's tough on the house. He pees on the oriental rugs with alarming casualness and he has shredded the screen on the back door.

He chews through computer cords, pulls

telephone wires from the wall. I catch him running from the living room with an extension cord in his mouth, and arrive just in time to catch the television it's attached to as it teeters from its perch.

And it's not just that he's a puppy; he's a very large puppy who's growing at an alarming rate. Each week he gains ten pounds of pure muscle. When the doorbell rings, he acts as if he's on angel dust and it takes all my strength to restrain him. If he squirms from my arms, visitors find themselves face-to-face with this leaping, exuberant adult-sized puppy dying for a piece of them.

It's 3 a.m. and I'm standing in the rain begging Fletcher to please go pee. His tail wagging, he splashes through the puddles, jumps for my umbrella, and then looking up, he tries to eat the falling raindrops.

I am not amused. A rivulet of cold water runs off the umbrella and trickles down the back of my shirt. Cross-eyed with fatigue, my patience has officially run out. I head to the door and call him, but of course, he ignores me and disappears into the bushes.

"You'll love having a puppy." Yeah, right.

But then, at 20 weeks old, a miracle begins. With each passing day, fewer shoes are chewed. He sleeps through the night. Fletcher begins to mellow—ever so slightly. It's been ten days since he last pranced through the house with an unraveling stream of toilet paper following him.

We are learning and he is learning. In the kitchen, he lies on his back. With his paws up and his mouth hanging open, he looks like a bat. I rub his stomach, and instead of biting my hand, he just lies there content. His hind leg starts to pump and he looks adoringly up at me. "Such a good boy," I say as I reluctantly give in to the first pangs of love.

A Slice of Turkey

Thanksgiving has always been a day of rushing—first to my in-laws', then to my sister's or mother's. Our visits have always had the distracted, clock-watching feel of a campaign stop.

"Hello, everybody. Great to see you. Pass the gravy. Got to go."

This year is different. We can finally stay put. For the first time ever, Thanksgiving is at our house.

Once the decision is made to host, my wife suddenly becomes Mother Teresa and wants to feed the world. Linda invites not just family, but friends of family, and the family of friends, and friends who are neighbors. The list expands and suddenly, thirty-four people are coming for dinner.

A subtle panic sets in. Linda paces the house, trying to visualize where people will sit, how traffic will flow, where the bar should go. Her sentences begin calmly enough, but end sounding like Sam Kinison with the hysterical refrain, "I'M COOKING FOR THIRTY-FOUR PEOPLE!!!"

She makes lists. Then lists of lists.

I, on the other hand, remain blissfully unaffected by it all. All I have to do is perform a few simple tasks on a checklist Linda has given me, and be dressed and have the puppy under control at four o'clock Thanksgiving Day.

An hour before the guests arrive, the puppy, now sixty pounds at six months old, becomes triple-espresso hyper. As I kneel to start the fire, he jumps on me and tries to bite my ears. When I toss him off, his attention turns to the firewood. He grabs a piece of oak and runs through the house, chewing it like a bone.

I need to wear him out fast. So I take him for a four-mile jog. By the time we arrive home, it's ten minutes to 4.

With my side of the family, this is no problem. They are dependably tardy, running about a time zone behind schedule. For them, four o'clock really means five-ish. But Linda's family has the unsettling habit of punctuality. When her parents arrive, I'm upstairs in the bathroom with a face full of shaving cream.

Far from being tired out by the run, the dog is energized. When Linda's parents walk through the door, their arms full of platters and dishes, he jumps like he's on a trampoline. Through the bathroom door I hear the commotion. Linda yells for me. I run downstairs in my bathrobe and grab the dog, apologizing and saying hello all at the same time. This is not an auspicious start.

I finish getting dressed, and the other guests start to arrive—my sister Katie, her husband and their five kids. Later, my brother Jim arrives with his wife and their five kids. Soon the house is as crowded as a college kegger. Guests need to step sideways to pass through the crowd.

With all parties, there is a physical center of gravity—usually the kitchen. For this one it's the den, where the bar and the buffet are set up. Packed in the space I find myself for the first time on the same eye level as my nephews and nieces. The former rug rats are suddenly young adults.

There's Peter and Kyle, both over six feet tall, and the statuesque Elizabeth, who looks to be almost as tall. Standing among the young giants, I feel like I'm sinking in soft sand.

I've tied the dog to a leg of the desk and he's unhappy about this. Pouting, he lies with his snout on his front paws. As he is surrounded by a forest of legs, high-heeled shoes come perilously close to his floppy ears, which are spread out on the floor, but he never flinches. Finally, he goes to sleep.

There is a tug at my shirt sleeve. It's my nephew, Charlie. Good old Charlie, he's still a little boy. Clutching a football as if it were his pillow, he asks if I can throw passes to him and his brother, Michael.

We step out to the backyard. In the vanishing light, the world is drained of color except for the browns and the grays and the dull green of the lawn. The frozen, bare earth is ready for winter.

Charlie runs out and I toss him a pass as soft as I can. The ball, nearly the size of his torso, knocks him off his feet, and his shoulder jams into the hard ground. I cringe at the pain such a fall would have caused me.

"Charlie, you OK?"

But he springs to his feet as if nothing has happened. The amazingly malleable, Rubbermaid body of youth is unaffected.

The boys run out for passes with the endless energy of retrievers chasing sticks. Between each play, a breathless Michael relates to me the intricate details of some distant, vaguely defined ball game.

"And then, and then, Uncle Bill, the score was tied. And like, and like this guy on the other team goes for the ball and, so I run and I'm like…"

He throws himself to the ground, apparently

re-enacting the great event. I guess as to when I should inject an enthusiastic, "Really, Michael. You don't say!!"

I try to get his wandering mind refocused on our little pass-and-catch drill.

"OK, Michael, this time go 10 yards and cut right."

He runs out and wanders off to the left. My pass disappears into the bushes, and darkness ends our game. We head back into the warmth of the house.

In the kitchen, the rich smells of turkey and dressing hang in the air. Linda and her mother stand by the stove, debating gravy strategy. Corn starch or flour?

In the living room, I jostle the fire and sit down with the older boys, who are sprawled on the couch watching football. I quiz Andy, a veritable ESPN SportsCenter of information. "What's the Cowboys' record?"

"7 and 3," he says without hesitation. "They've won their last three in a row."

Turning to Conner, who is in eighth grade, I ask the typical, annoying questions that adults tend to ask. Each elicits a monotone, one-syllable reply:

"How's school?"

"Fine," he says without enthusiasm.

"How's swimming?"

His wide eyes remain glued to the game. "Good."

Grace is somehow said above the raucous din, and dinner is served. People wander the house with loaded plates looking for seats. Besides the kitchen and dining room, they sit in improbable locations, perched on the arms of occupied chairs, in the basement next to my weight set, and in front of the bay window in the living room.

I sit with my nieces. Precocious Mary, now in fifth grade, shows off her sophistication by beginning her sentences with the very grown-up word "actually." Her sisters, Emily and Caroline, who the day before swam in the state high school swim meet, describe a workout schedule I can't fathom.

Elizabeth, now a freshman in college, has developed a dry wit. She earnestly compliments me on my cooking and the centerpieces without a trace of a smile. "Uncle Bill, I have no idea how you do it all. You're just amazing."

After dinner we assemble everyone for pictures. While the old folks study cameras through bifocals, trying to figure out which buttons to push, the kids grow restless. Baby Faith and toddler Blake squirm in their mother's arms. Directions are screamed at the photographers. Pictures are taken but heads are cut off and cameras malfunction.

A riot is about to ensue when, finally, the flash goes off, and everyone is miraculously in frame, looking at the camera. The precious chaos is captured, this transitory moment between childhood and adulthood, middle and old age, life and death. And like a flash, the moment vanishes and becomes but a memory.

Paris 1983

T his is my last grand adventure before entering
the real, suit-and-tie world of practicing law. I
have two months before I start my job. Until then,
it's just me and my backpack traveling across
Europe. I am completely unprepared. I have no
idea where I'm going or what I'm doing.

I've just arrived in Paris and I'm sitting at an
outdoor café trying to figure out where I am, and
where I'm going to spend the night. A middle-aged
American who reminds me of Tim Conway strolls
by. He wears a loud blue golf shirt, white shorts
pulled up to his chest, white knee-high socks
and brand new tennis shoes. Around his neck is
a camera, and under his arms he clutches a stack
of tour books. He spots an empty table next to
mine.

His tour books topple off the table as he anxiously waves at the waiter. "Ah, Gar sun?" he says in a voice that trails off like he's talking to himself.

When the curt, impatient waiter finally arrives, the man haltingly orders in English, but with a French accent. The waiter offers a brief, pained smile as if he can barely endure the experience of taking the man's order. He snatches the menu from the unworthy American and disappears in a huff. I feel embarrassed for my countryman, and within five minutes, we strike up a conversation. I pick his brain on where to stay and what to see.

Ted is his name, a bachelor from Dubuque. He recommends his hotel as the best value he could find. I figure with the library of tour books he's carrying, he has to know what he's talking about. So I thank him for the tip and later that day check in for a night at the reasonably priced hotel in the Latin Quarter. That evening, I bump into Ted in the lobby.

"Hey, stranger!" he says. He now wears a sweater tied around his neck as if he's off to play a game of doubles. "Say, I'm headed up to Montmartre this evening. Why don't you join me?"

Ted is the last person I want to spend time with in Paris. I stutter and stammer as I try to invent an excuse, but I feel socially indebted to him for the lead on this fine hotel.

"Um, yeah, sure," I say with an absence of enthusiasm I hope isn't too obvious.

As we take the cab up the hill to Montmartre, Ted studies his maps and tour books. We get out of the cab, wander around for a while and finally stop in a bar where we are warmly greeted at the door by two burly bouncers.

It's early, so we're the only ones in the place. We sit down and soon two beautiful women come out of nowhere and sit at our sides. A bucket of ice and champagne arrives. "Who ordered that?" I ask Ted.

"Who cares?" he says, gleefully toasting me with his glass.

The women giggle and flirt with us and sip their champagne. It all seems a little too good to be true. Soon a second bottle of champagne arrives that neither of us ordered. I jump out of my seat.

"Ted, we got to get out of here."

But Ted is now glassy-eyed and deliriously excited by the woman at his side who is stroking his hair and purring French in his ear. "But the girls want us to go upstairs with them," he says, his eyebrows arching lecherously.

"Listen, Ted. We didn't order the champagne. They're setting us up. We're being ripped off. Let's get out of here." The girl at his side suddenly glares up at me.

Ted is not listening. I head for the door without him, but the manager steps in my way and presents me with a bill for the champagne. It's nearly $200. I tell him we didn't order the champagne and we're not paying for it. He is joined by the two bouncers.

"You pay for the champagne!" he demands. When I refuse, he claps his hands and one of the bouncers reaches behind the bar and pulls out an empty champagne bottle the size of a Louisville slugger and hands it to the manager, who grabs it with both hands around the neck and rests it on his shoulders. "You will pay!!!" he screams.

I contemplate making a dash for the door, but one of the bouncers shifts to block the exit. The women have now disappeared and Ted is so scared he's ready to wet his pants. "Let's just pay!" he pleads.

Reluctantly, I pay my half with a credit card, fuming as I sign the receipt. I'm mad at myself and mad at Ted for allowing us to be victims of this high-class mugging. We ride back to the city in silence in the back of the cab.

The next day things improve. I visit the American Express office and explain what happened, and they agree to forgive the charge. And that evening I meet a Parisian woman named Fabian. She's 19, pretty, and best of all, she has a friend who's out of town for the month and is letting her stay at her place in exchange for taking care of her cat. "My apartment is free. Why don't you stay there?" she asks in broken English. So now I have a free place to stay in Paris. What could be better?

The days pass, and I meet Fabian's friends; I find myself insinuated into her social circle, going to parties, playing tennis and taking bicycle rides and picnics in the country. It's all very nice, but there's one problem: I'm here to see Europe, not Fabian. So after a couple of weeks I pack my bag and thank her for everything and try to explain that I am leaving to see the rest of Europe.

I don't understand her French, but I get her meaning. There is screaming and tears and a door slams behind me as I slink off into the night like a stray cat.

I take a train to Germany, and then Italy and Greece. After six weeks, I return to Paris one last night before flying back to the United States. I'm short on money, but I don't dare call Fabian. To save money so I can go out for the evening, I check into a youth hostel.

It is a warm night as I walk through the Left Bank and there is excitement in the air. On Boulevard St. Michele, a fight breaks out between a British and a French couple. The two men punch and flail at each other for about a minute before falling on top of each other in an exhausted heap.

The police easily separate them.

But the women have a hold of each other's hair and they scream and tear at each other's clothes as their battle goes from one side of the street to the other. A delighted crowd gathers to watch the spectacle. One of the officers attempts to intervene but is clawed in the face. His partner has to help out. He reaches around the waist of the French woman and pulls her away kicking and cursing. A high-heel shoe is flung angrily off her foot and lands in the middle of the street.

I walk up the Latin Quarter and wander down a narrow street and into an obscure tiny nightclub. I notice a door at the back of the club that leads down an ancient staircase. I follow the music into a cave-like sub-basement room.

Through the haze of smoke, on the stage I see a beautiful, willowy black woman. She sings a languid, sultry version of that sappy love song by Eric Carmen, "All By Myself." As she sings, she presses her hands against the low stone ceiling, and writhes seductively. In front of me, a man pulls out a knife and cuts a chunk of hash, which he places in a pipe, lights and passes around.

By the time I stagger back to the hostel, I've missed the curfew by about three hours and the place is locked up for the night. My backpack is inside and I'm desperate for a place to sleep. I bang on the doors and somehow convince the angry attendant to let me in.

I make my way upstairs to the room where I left my stuff. The air is close and alive with the sounds of men snoring in their bunks. I stumble and grope my way through the darkness to my bed. As I undress, I reflect on what a wonderful adventure I've had these last two months.

I pull off my shirt and dive into bed, my bare chest landing on the equally bare chest of a man who leaps up and screams at me in what I think is Arabic. The entire hostel erupts, and lights are turned on. I stand there, the stupid American in his underwear apologizing to twelve angry men.

That was the last time I was in Paris.

And now, nearly a quarter century later, our plane descends into Charles de Gaulle airport. I close the tour book in my lap, and take my wife's hand as our plane touches down with a jolt.

Introspection

The door to the waiting room opens and the nurse calls out, "William White? William?"

The formal version of my name makes my stomach tighten. It's always a serious matter when I'm called William. It reminds me of being summoned into the principal's office.

My wife squeezes my hand.

"Are you sure you don't mind waiting?" I ask.

"I have plenty of work to do," she says. "Good luck."

I follow the nurse through a labyrinth of examination rooms and stations, to a little changing room covered by a curtain.

"You can put your clothes in here," she says, handing me a plastic bag. "Then put these on."

A few minutes later I emerge wearing a

279

light fabric backless gown and little booty socks with rubber padded non-slip soles. God I hope I don't bump into anyone I know. The nurse has me follow her again. I double-check my ties in back as we go deeper into the medical maze, this time down a hall to a corner room where the examination will take place.

Even though I'm here for a routine colonoscopy, I feel like I'm Gary Gilmore being led to his execution.

She hooks me up to a monitor that displays my vital signs.

"The doctor will be in shortly."

My stomach growls angrily with nothing to do. This is day two without food. Between fasting and the startlingly effective laxatives I took last night, my system has been emptied like a stadium after a home team loss.

I lie on the table staring up at the rectangle panels of fluorescent lights. As if a ghost has entered the room, the blood pressure cuff on my arm suddenly begins to tighten. It squeezes until the creepy throbbing sensation runs down my arm and a new set of readings is displayed on the monitor.

I look around the room. Everything is beige. Institutional beige. There is nothing to look at or read except the instructions in three languages on the rubber glove dispenser mounted on the wall.

Where is the doctor?

I play a game with the heart monitor. My pulse rate is fifty. Can I lower it? I breathe slowly and meditate and get it down to 46. Okay. I'm bored with that game.

It's been a half hour.

Out in the hall, the health care workers in their jogging shoes hurry by. They look stressed. I think about our health care system. Do these workers have time to care? What will the state of health care be when I'm 60, 70 and 80? Does anyone remember I'm in here? It's been nearly an hour.

I just turned 50—the age of AARP mailings and colonoscopies. It's hard to believe I've reached what once seemed like such a distant and mythical age.

I remember when my dad turned 50. Neighbors put a big banner across the front lawn: "Bob White is 50!" it said; kind of like, ha, ha, you're old. I got the same treatment at work. A big poster on my door, signed by the staff offering their condolences.

Then I remember my dad had colon cancer in the early '80s. He recovered fully, but the thought is sobering. I'm suddenly a little nervous. Anxious. Where the hell is the doctor?

My pulse shoots up to 60. I think about mortality. Turning 50 is like the changing of the first leaves in late summer. The weather is still fine but the days are noticeably shorter.

So what happens when we die? And what is the meaning of this life beyond the paychecks and oil changes and the physical things of this world? My dad was an old-school Catholic—daily Mass and Rosary and acts of charity. Throughout his life he had certainty. And in the end, at age 81, he had peace. His religion served him well.

But me, I'm not so religious; on the other hand, I'm not non-religious either. I'm like a spiritual hedge fund with a balanced portfolio of faith and reason. And because I know my mortal mind can never explain all of life's mysteries, I don't rule anything out.

A nurse walks by and I call out. She doesn't hear me. It's like I'm a helpless resident in a nursing home crying out to no avail.

Another nurse finally enters the room, apologizing that it has taken so long. She explains that they had to call an interpreter in for one patient, and the next patient was elderly and the procedure took much longer than expected.

I beg her for something to read, anything.

She returns with an old tattered copy of *US Weekly*, apologizing that it's the only thing she could find. But I am grateful to have something to pass the time, and I eagerly devour the insider story of Jessica Simpson and Nick Lachey's divorce.

At last, the doctor enters the room and adds to

the chorus of apologies. He's a fairly young man but he looks tired, like he hasn't seen sunlight in years. His thinning blonde hair lays across his head like cut straw.

"How are we doing today?" he asks, snapping on rubber gloves.

"Not bad. Although I'm a little depressed over Nick and Jessica breaking up," I say, pointing at the magazine.

The nurse prepares to inject something into my veins.

"Do you have someone to drive you home?" she asks. "Because you won't want to be operating any heavy machinery or making any big decisions for the rest of the day."

The needle goes in and the effect is immediate, non-subtle and oh-so-narcotic. Suddenly the world seems positively swell. I look at the nurse. I think I love her. And the doctor. They are about to put a garden hose up my rear and I could care less.

"Hey Doc. You, know, I don't feel so bad about Jessica and whass-his-face anymore."

"I figured you'd feel better. Now, we're going to have you roll over on your side. If you want you can watch the monitor.

"Well, look what's on TV," I say. I watch with fascination the dark, mysterious and serpentine journey to the center of my being. The light from the scope casts eerie shadows, like a miner's lamp on the walls of a cave. Talk about introspection. What an age we live in.

The exam takes only about fifteen minutes. There's little, if any discomfort.

"Clean as a whistle," the doctor says. "Everything looks fine. You won't have to do this for another seven to ten years."

I feel elated. Like I've been given a new lease on life.

Linda drives me home, and on the way we stop at Starbucks. The first sip of coffee nearly brings me to my knees. At home we have lunch and I savor the taste of the first solid food in forty hours. Perhaps it's the drugs, but I am overwhelmed with gratitude. For the bread, a simple cup of coffee. My wife and my life. Even for Fletcher, who runs off with my napkin.

Fifty years old. From here on, I'm in the bonus zone, baby.

Stray Cats

E vening light slants through the neighborhood. Sprinklers hiss and their spray is made brilliant by the dazzling sunlight. Roy and I stand in the street, pounding our gloves, waiting for Craig to hit us the next fly ball.

With a Wilson tennis racquet Craig smacks a ball into the stratosphere. The ball hangs motionless in the sky before beginning its descent to earth.

Craig does the play-by-play announcing: "Way back, way back, to the warning track!"

I make the catch just before plowing into the Andersons' hedge, our imaginary outfield wall.

Sitting on her front steps, Roy's mother sets down her cigarette and applauds.

She has just fixed a cocktail for herself and the dour-faced Ted Stevens from across the street.

They drink from candy-colored tin tumblers that sweat with the July humidity.

Roy's mother is not like the others in this Edina neighborhood. She is an artist—an actress at the Old Log Theater. She doesn't cook or clean or play tennis or do anything remotely suburban. She spends her days perched on the couch, shades drawn against the daylight, smoking cigarettes like a silent movie star and watching her soap operas.

"Billy White, I want you to sit down here and tell me ALL ABOUT SCHOOL," she'd say, in her husky Bette Davis voice, projecting as if she were trying to be heard in the back row of some darkened theater.

I would sit down on the worn davenport and relate the trouble I was in with the nuns at school. This delighted her. And when the commercial was over, and her soap opera came back on, Roy and I would sneak out the door, on to our next adventure.

Dusk descends on the neighborhood. The cigarettes glow and the mosquitoes come out. Ted Stevens finishes his drink and stands up stiffly, patting his belly as he says good-bye to Roy's mom. He passes through our game glum-faced without saying a word, back to his house across the street.

Now it is dark, and the object of our game is to catch Craig's towering shots as they descend out of the night sky and into the glow of the streetlights. After a half hour of this near-impossible game, we call it a day. Tomorrow we'll think of something else to do. But we won't think of that until tomorrow arrives.

But the next morning, my mother nearly ruins the potential for fun. She rouses me out of bed early and gives me a list of chores to do.

"Aw, Mom!" I whine.

My complaining sets her off. "Bob Jim Jean Kate," she stammers through most of her six children's names, until finally arriving at mine. "Bah Bile, Bill! I want you out of that bed, I want the house to be…and the garage needs…"

I can tell she means business because when she's upset she has the habit of speaking in one endless run-on sentence.

"I want you to sweep, and there's leaves in the gutters that need to be, no, and your room, I don't want you lollygagging, and, yes, bring your dirty laundry, so I can start the machine, and the garbage out…and, no, I want your bed made and, yes, this is not a boarding house, young man."

While I'm on the roof dejectedly pulling leaves from the gutters, Roy and Craig come over. They lie next to their bikes on our front lawn and watch me work. We try to decide what to do with our day.

Should we climb the light towers at the high school football field? Should we throw rocks at the carp in the creek? But we've done all that. We need to do something new.

Looking at their bikes, I hit upon the idea. Let's ride our bikes to the Twins game.

I quickly finish my work, put away the ladder and grab my bike. There is no need to tell my mother where I'm going. I'm 12 years old and perfectly able to take care of myself. And besides, I'm afraid she'll give me more work.

We take off on our journey, not knowing the way, just the direction. We make our way past Southdale, and along the frontage roads of 494, until finally, in the distance, we see the colored checkers of Metropolitan Stadium rising from the midday heat like a mirage. We made it!

We lock our bikes outside of left field, and for $2.50 we buy tickets in the bleachers. Our seats are in the upper deck, near the seat marking Harmon Killebrew's longest homerun.

We watch batting practice for a while before realizing these seats may be good for football, but for baseball we might as well be in the next county. The game would be a distant event.

So we leave the bleachers and try to sneak into the seats along the left field foul line. We are quickly removed by the usher, who tells us to go back to the bleachers.

Then I get another idea. "Let's crawl under the stands."

The great thing about Roy and Craig is they are game for anything. Without hesitation, we look around, and seeing no one coming, we hop a fence and crawl like Marines through the gravel and discarded plastic cups and Frosty Malt lids all the way up to the field next to the third-base dugout. These are the best seats in the house and no one knows we're under here!

With our faces pressed against the chain-link fence, we watch the Oakland A's take batting practice. Reggie Jackson and Sal Bando walk past. We can hear the players needling each other and the sounds of their metal cleats as they descend into the dugout.

We look at each other. "This is so cool!"

A pair of loafers appears in front of us. I look up and see Tony Kubek, the former Yankee short-stop who is now the color man for the NBC game of the week. He is preparing to do an interview. He takes his mark inches in front of us.

There is a great commotion from the stands above us as a pair of white cleats joins the loafers for the interview. I look up to see who it is. The face is as recognizable as any on Mount Rushmore.

We look up in awe as the shadow of Joe DiMaggio falls upon us.

"Hey, Joe. Joe. Joe. We love you!!!" The fans cry out from above.

He wears number 5, but to see the Yankee

Clipper in the silly green and gold uniform of the A's seems to be a desecration of an American icon. He deserves the dignity of pinstripes, whether they be on a suit or a baseball uniform.

Nevertheless, I take in the moment and contemplate the significance of the famous feet before me. The fifty-six-game hitting streak. The graceful centerfielder. Marilyn Monroe. Mr. Coffee.

On our way home, we think of the next adventure. "Hey, let's see if we can go a week without going indoors. We'll call it 'survival camp.' We can camp in the woods behind our house and build fires and cook our meals. You guys in?"

Craig and Roy look at me like I've asked the silliest question in the world. "Why not?" they say. To us at that moment, it seems there is nothing in the world we can't do.

Of Bats and Men

My wife nudges me. "Honey, wake up!"

I'm having such a nice dream. I try to ignore her, but she persists.

"Listen…do you hear that? There's something flying around in here!"

I roll over, fluffing my pillow. "Probly jussa moth," I say dreamily. I'm hoping I can pick up where I left off in the dream I was having.

"Don't worry. It'll fly away," I say vaguely. "Less talk about it inna morning, 'kay?" I drift back to sleep.

"Bill!!!" she says, shaking me like a martini. "I think it's a bat!!!"

I sit up, rubbing my eyes, wondering why she insists on torturing me like this. The clock says 2:14 a.m.

"Aw, honey, it's nothing," I whine. "Look, I'll prove it."

I reach over and flip on the light. "See?"

The light comes on with the jolting effect of a camera flash. I look up just in time to see a bat, which to my terrified eyes looks to be the size of a bald eagle. It swoops down upon us and we both fall back on the pillows like a pair of batters ducking a high inside fastball.

"Holy #!@$!!!" I say, now fully awake.

"Some moth," my wife says.

The creature circles again, its shadow stretching along the ceiling. The breeze from its wings can be felt as it swoops perilously close to our faces.

Is there something wrong with his sonar? He shouldn't be coming this close to us. I roll out of bed onto the floor, and crawl towards the door.

"Stay here," I say unnecessarily to my wife, who has disappeared under two pillows and the covers she's pulled over her head. She makes a muffled, urgent sound in response.

The dog is excitedly leaping for the bat. Snapping in vain at the airborne object, his teeth make a chomping sound like dentures. I grab him by the collar and drag him out of the room and throw him in the bathroom.

I poke my head back in the bedroom door. "Don't worry, honey," I say, trying to conceal the shaking in my voice and my fear of bats.

"It's just a little bat. There's nothing to be afraid—Whoooaaaahhhh!!!"

The bat swoops toward me and I drop to my knees. I grab a pillow and start swinging at it like a schoolgirl at a pajama party. I hit nothing but the light fixture. This is not my most manly moment. With the chandelier swinging and my wife yelling and the dog barking, even the bat can't stand the commotion. He exits the room and flies downstairs.

I stand at the top of the stairs, my heart crashing in my chest and my brain racing through its very limited catalog of "What to do if a bat is flying around your house." Visions of tennis rackets, buckets, album covers, fishnets and shovels run through my panicked head.

I tear through my closet searching for my tennis racket, but it's been years since I've played. Maybe it's in the garage or the basement. At any rate, I don't have time to look.

Staying close to the wall, I cautiously make my way down the stairs like a TV cop, one step at a time. I flip on the lights. The bat is bobbing and weaving around the dining room table.

I run through the house, shutting every door I can to contain and limit the flight options of our visitor. Meanwhile, my wife tiptoes down the stairs with the dog and goes to her computer in the den, where she Googles "bat removal."

In the kitchen I search for the appropriate implement. I toss spatulas and spoons and frying pans aside and emerge with my weapon of choice: a cookie sheet. I step into the dining room and wait for the bat to come my way. I swing wildly and miss. It's like trying to hit a knuckleball on a windy day. I swing again. And again. All to no avail.

"Open the front door!" my wife yells from her computer. "It says they'll sense the fresh air and fly out the door."

I open the front door and return to the dining room. Where did it go, I wonder? Did it fly out already? My wife enters cautiously.

"There it is," she says, pointing at the window. Clinging high on the curtain with its wings contracted, the bat now appears to be no larger than an egg.

I cautiously approach, taking half steps like a fencer in a duel. I delicately touch the curtain. But he does not move. I poke a little higher. Still no movement. Then I gently nudge him with the cookie sheet. His wings begin to spread like a vampire.

I step away quickly and try to regather my composure. This time I poke him more forcefully and he goes airborne again. I start swinging the cookie sheet like a madman and issuing irrational, incomprehensible orders at my wife and the dog.

"Get the!!! Move!!! Don't let him!!! Watch out!!!"

The bat circles and circles, but won't head for the door. With each lap he seems to tire and move a little slower. Finally, he flies into my wheelhouse. I take a mighty swing and make solid contact. The bat ricochets off the ceiling and skids across the polished wood until it comes to rest at the head of the table.

I've killed him. I didn't mean to, but I did.

I bend over to inspect the body. Poor little fella. He didn't want to hurt anybody; he just got confused. I feel a pang of sorrow and regret.

Suddenly, he begins to stir. I stumble backward, half relieved and half terrified.

He flaps his wings and performs a sort of breaststroke across the table, before dropping out of sight onto one of the chairs. I pull out the chair. Lying on the seat of the chair, he's spreading his wings, about to take flight.

I race for the front door, crashing one of the chair legs against the doorway as I make my way outside. On the front sidewalk, I give a mighty heave and send the bat flying off into the night.

And just like that, the battle is over. I, the triumphant man, stand on the sidewalk in my underwear, holding a chair. Breathless from the great battle, I take a moment to savor this 21st-century suburban victory over nature.

I breathe in the thrilling night air before going

inside. Lights are turned off and the front door is locked. Outside the crickets roar and the darkness teems with unseen life.

Stark Waving Mad

Outside, in the darkness, danger lurks. With tiny, careful steps, an elderly woman and her dog shuffle along up our street. She is deaf. The dog is blind.

My wife and I don't grasp the situation. Only our dog, Fletcher, fully comprehends the threat this menacing pair poses to our safety and well-being.

Fletcher, our 14-month-old Black Lab-Husky mix, who has the body of a linebacker and the mind of a puppy, sits intently alert at our front bay window, his anxious breath frosting the glass. He is not at all pleased that this woman and her dog would dare to walk in front of his house.

Grrrrrrrrrrrr. Grrrrrrrrrrrr.

He registers his disapproval with a low

growl that rumbles in his chest like a distant, approaching storm. He shifts nervously from one haunch to the other.

Before the rattling growl erupts into a bark, I try to distract him. The dog needs exercise. He always needs exercise. We can't walk him enough.

So I grab his leash from the closet, and suddenly become the most fascinating person on earth. He watches me intently, following me from one room to the next as I put on a sweater, and gather hat and gloves and plastic bags.

He begins hyperventilating. Will he be left behind? His nervousness translates into a yawn. His long tongue rolls out of his mouth like a red carpet.

He paces, and then begins to audition. He sits, lies down, and sits again. The suspense overwhelms him, and he begins to whimper and whine.

Finally the torture ends as I finish getting dressed. We make our way out the door onto the street. The cold night air is rich with the smell of birch and oak burning in someone's fireplace. On young legs, Fletcher prances like a show dog; his head is on swivel checking out the neighborhood.

He veers off to visit all the usual rest stops: the hydrant, the tree, the lamppost. On this December evening, without leaves on the trees or snow on the ground, the frozen earth lies bare beneath the crystal moon.

A car drives by slowly as if the occupants are inspecting us. I can't make out who is behind the darkened windows, but I wave anyway. It's a defensive wave; insurance against snubbing someone I should acknowledge. I figure, what's the downside? When in doubt, wave.

I wait for Fletcher. And wait. And finally I pull him from a shrub as he balances on one leg, trying to eke out one last drop. When he finishes, he rakes the lawn with his back legs, tossing clumps of grass and dirt onto the street, before resuming his eager journey.

Up ahead, comes the young blonde mother from down the street who power walks past our house every day. Now you'd think, just looking at her, that she'd be a waver. But my wife and I have waved at her numerous times, only to be ignored. I give this woman the benefit of the doubt. Maybe she doesn't have her contacts in or is lost in her iTunes.

This time, however, she has to see me. I'm under a street light, directly in her line of travel. If I don't move, she'll run into me. I grab hold of the dog, who will leap without notice into the face of any stranger. When only a few feet separate us I give her a big smile and wave.

"Hello. Nice night," I say loud enough to be heard over her earphones.

But my greeting is a social air ball. It falls to the street unanswered and rolls to the gutter. Nothing. Not a smile, nor a nod. Not even a shifting of the eyes in my direction. She marches past stolid as a Buckingham Palace guard.

As I walk along I contemplate the non-waver. She is among a rare and special breed. Like those people you hold the door for, who walk past without acknowledging the gesture. How do they do it?

I have a certain respect for this level of antisocial will power. The discipline it must take to not allow the head to nod, or a smile to form, or a one-syllable "thanks" or "hi" to pass the lips.

We continue our walk. In the living rooms giant high-definition TVs broadcast to us that in this house, they are watching *America's Next Top Model*, and in that house, it's Bears 13, Packers 7 with 3:17 left in the second quarter. I could pull a chair up in the middle of the street and see these screens better than I can see ours from the couch at home.

Down the street I see the happy, precision-walking husband and wife team. Perhaps in their early seventies and beaming with good health, they look like they walked out of a Citracal commercial. As if on cue, they both give me identical smiles and synchronized waves. The neighborly greeting executed to perfection.

We make our way out of the neighborhood and walk the street next to the highway. The houses here are modest, post-WWII bungalows with one-car garages.

A man stands on the front steps of one of these homes blowing cigarette smoke at the moon. Banished from the house, the brave smoker endures the cold without a jacket.

Being nearly a half-mile from home, I suppose I'm well outside the mandatory wave zone. But it's the Minnesotan in me. I feel compelled. I have to wave.

With hands jammed in his pockets, and the cigarette clenched in his teeth, the man squints through the smoke to see if he recognizes me. Looking slightly perplexed, he hesitantly returns the gesture by tossing his head back, as if he were swallowing a pill.

We circle back to our neighborhood, and Fletcher still wants to stop at every tree and bush. How does he not run dry?

As we turn the corner for our house, I see the elderly woman and her blind dog now making their way back down our street. The woman's flashlight swings like a lantern. Fletcher's tail begins fanning wildly. He wants to greet the former enemies like long-lost friends.

He races for the woman, the leash running out like fishing line. When it comes to the end he nearly yanks my arm out of socket. He wants to play with the dog and jump into the arms of the woman.

I struggle to regain control and the old woman nearly stumbles over her dog. Even though she can't hear me, I apologize to her and pull Fletcher up our driveway scolding him as I go. I look again to see if she is OK. She stands in the street and ever so slowly, raises her hand and waves at us both.

Getting the Message

It's 2 a.m. and I cannot sleep. Instead of reading a book, or watching an old episode of *Columbo* on TV, I am drawn to the computer. I can't resist. I must check e-mail.

I open Outlook Express, and a sea of black and bold subject lines appears. Dozens upon dozens of unread e-mails wait for my attention.

This afternoon I made the mistake of spending several hours away from the computer. Instead of e-mailing, I was talking to people. And planning and reflecting. Silly me. While I was doing this, e-mails multiplied in my inbox like rabbits.

Now, instead of Hail Marys, my penance is 107 e-mails. I begin the long, slow crawl through the messages. There are the easy ones, those that offer a lower-interest rate, a better sex life, the next hot stock. These I eliminate quickly. And then it's down to business.

An hour and a half later, I'm still inching my way to the top of the screen. Only a dozen messages to go. Bah bing. Two more spam e-mails appear. Bah bing. Headlines from the *Star Tribune*. Bah bing. Another newsletter. I feel like a swimmer trying to get to shore, only to be pulled out to sea by the tide. Or Hercules battling the Hydra. I cut off a head only to have two more appear.

But finally, I make it to the top of the page. I've done it. A clean, pristine inbox. I feel a euphoric sense of control and completion. Now I can sleep.

I get up and make my way back to bed. But as I walk out of the den, I hear another Bah bing. Like one of Pavlov's dogs hearing the bell, I am programmed to respond. I turn around and head back to the computer.

A co-worker has replied to one of my e-mails—at 3:30 a.m.! It's eerie and unnerving to know there is someone else out there at this hour—like having a face suddenly appear at the window.

I do not want to start an e-mail volley at this hour, so I resist the temptation to respond and head up to bed. While I sleep, the steady and inexorable accretion of messages begins anew.

At the office in the morning, besides a fresh

batch of e-mails, there are the voicemails. These fall into several categories:

The life story voice mails: Way, way more information than is needed; these callers have difficulty getting to the point; they make several failed attempts to wrap up the message before being mercifully cut off.

The no-rhythm messages: These people have trouble with the basic cadence of a phone number, grouping the digits in odd ways that make the number nearly indecipherable: "So gimme a call at 3...128...26...364...5."

The everyone-knows-who-I-am voice messages: Some callers believe there's no need to repeat or spell their name or even to say it clearly because everyone knows them. Sometimes they feel it is unnecessary to leave their phone numbers.

Death bed messages: These people sound as if they lack the will to live, much less to leave a clear and coherent message. The act of leaving a message drains their life force, so by the time it comes to leaving their phone number, they are mumbling inaudibly. I'm left yelling at the phone, "34 what??!!! What!!! Say it again!!!"

On the way home, I check my BlackBerry. Since I left the office, twelve e-mails and four voice messages have arrived.

I walk in the door and get back on the computer and begin cleaning up my inbox when my wife walks in the door.

"Have you checked messages?" she asks, referring to the home phone.

Who is she kidding? I don't even know how to retrieve messages from the home phone. Why do I want to? I've got enough messages.

She plays the voicemails.

There are two hang-ups from solicitors, and then, a message from my mother.

"It's Mom calling."

Even though a mother's voice is the most recognizable on earth, there is a universal principle that all mothers need to identify themselves when leaving phone messages.

"Billy boy, darling. Just calling to see how you're feeling. I hope your cold is better."

Another universal principle: If you've been sick, this causes a mother to address you as if you're 6 years old.

"And lovely Linda, thank you for that beautiful scarf. I'm wearing it right now as I speak." Unbeknown to me, we gave her the scarf for her 84th birthday.

"And thank you both for the wonderful dinner the other night." Again, something I had nothing to do with. My mother has already sent us a thank-you note—the old-fashioned handwritten kind with the flawless cursive and heart-felt eloquence. No hurried lower-case e-mail from her.

"Sorry to bother you two. No need to call." She always says this.

"Oh, and Bill, remind me to tell you. I saw the best movie the other night. There was a little bit of vulgar language that they could have done without ..." Almost all her reviews contain a similar disclaimer about the language or violence "they could have done without."

"But oh, what a story!" My mother is the family arts and entertainment critic. She's always going to the latest play, movie, or museum opening. She's so busy it's hard to get on her schedule.

"And don't forget Thursday is a holy day of obligation.

"Oh, and I can't remember if I told you, but I went to Pat Murphy's funeral today. You remember Pat from my bridge club. In fact, she played with us two weeks ago. Well, she died on Saturday when she went out to pick up the morning paper. Nicest gal."

My poor mother needs a spreadsheet to keep track of her friends' funerals, fractures, cancers and strokes.

"Bye, bye. I love you two."

And that, the 127th message of the day, is the message that matters most.

Acknowledgements

T hanks to my family and friends, without whom I'd have no material; to my wife, Linda, who has been my most trusted editor on these stories, and a great sport for letting me write about her and her family. Thanks also to Deborah Rybak, for kicking me in the butt a few times to get this book done; Brett Johnson, who brought me into the magazine business and gave me free reign; Steve Kaplan and Adam Wahlberg, the brilliant editors of *Law & Politics*, who have gently and persistently pushed me along to write my column each issue, despite my whining and complaining; photographer Larry Marcus, with whom I've had the pleasure of working and creating *Law & Politics* covers for 20 years, and who took the photo for this book; Holly Dolezalek, who hand entered a decade's worth of columns because I couldn't locate the original electronic files; Aimée Groth, for her editorial assistance; Mike Maupin, for his advice and direction; Jessica Thompson, whose keen editorial eye helped save the day; and Vance Opperman, the generous and supportive owner of our magazines.

Printed in the United States
132198LV00007B/30/P